# CAMBRIDGE LIBRARY COLLECTION

*Books of enduring scholarly value*

## Travel, Europe

This collection of narratives contains vivid accounts of the varied landscapes, built environment and customs encountered by eighteenth- and nineteenth-century travellers in the British Isles and Europe. Some were wealthy individuals on the Grand Tour, while others were travelling on business, for pleasure, in pursuit of better health, or simply to escape trouble at home.

## Naples and Garibaldi

This short book derives from an article published in the periodical *Vacation Tourists and Notes of Travel*, edited by Francis Galton, in 1860. W.G. Clark (1821–78) was most famous as co-editor of the Cambridge Shakespeare, but was originally a classical scholar, whose *Peloponnesus* (1858) is also reissued in this series. This lively account of a critical period in Italian history, 'during the occurrence of events so strange and sudden that they resembled incidents of a romantic melodrama rather than real history', deliberately avoids the usual landscapes, ruins and peasants to give a day-by-day description of events in Naples at the time when Garibaldi had arrived in the city during his campaign for the liberation of the Kingdom of the Two Sicilies. However, as well as narrating political and military developments, Clark introduces some picturesque notes, including an account of the famous 'miracle' of the liquefaction of St Gennaro's blood.

Cambridge University Press has long been a pioneer in the reissuing of out-of-print titles from its own backlist, producing digital reprints of books that are still sought after by scholars and students but could not be reprinted economically using traditional technology. The Cambridge Library Collection extends this activity to a wider range of books which are still of importance to researchers and professionals, either for the source material they contain, or as landmarks in the history of their academic discipline.

Drawing from the world-renowned collections in the Cambridge University Library and other partner libraries, and guided by the advice of experts in each subject area, Cambridge University Press is using state-of-the-art scanning machines in its own Printing House to capture the content of each book selected for inclusion. The files are processed to give a consistently clear, crisp image, and the books finished to the high quality standard for which the Press is recognised around the world. The latest print-on-demand technology ensures that the books will remain available indefinitely, and that orders for single or multiple copies can quickly be supplied.

The Cambridge Library Collection brings back to life books of enduring scholarly value (including out-of-copyright works originally issued by other publishers) across a wide range of disciplines in the humanities and social sciences and in science and technology.

# Naples and Garibaldi

William George Clark

CAMBRIDGE
UNIVERSITY PRESS

CAMBRIDGE UNIVERSITY PRESS

Cambridge, New York, Melbourne, Madrid, Cape Town,
Singapore, São Paolo, Delhi, Mexico City

Published in the United States of America by Cambridge University Press, New York

www.cambridge.org
Information on this title: www.cambridge.org/9781108054768

© in this compilation Cambridge University Press 2013

This edition first published 1861
This digitally printed version 2013

ISBN 978-1-108-05476-8 Paperback

# VACATION TOURISTS

AND

## NOTES OF TRAVEL

IN 1860

EDITED BY

## FRANCIS GALTON, M.A. F.R.S.

AUTHOR OF "THE ART OF TRAVEL," ETC.

Cambridge

MACMILLAN AND CO

AND 23, HENRIETTA STREET, COVENT GARDEN

London

1861

# VACATION TOURISTS, &c. IN 1860.

## 1. *NAPLES AND GARIBALDI.*

### BY W. G. CLARK, M.A. F.R.G.S.

*Through Turin to Naples.*—I left London on the 18th of August, for the tour which has become a matter of annual recurrence. It had been my intention to go to Scotland, but the almost incessant rain which spoilt our last summer drove me to seek for sunshine in some southern land, and the interest attaching to Garibaldi's daring enterprise drew me irresistibly to Italy. The route from England to Naples, travelled every year by thousands of our countrymen and not new to myself, would, in ordinary circumstances, be too hackneyed a topic ; and a writer who should suppose that he had anything to say about it which had not been said before—the only justification for writing at all—would show great confidence in his own powers of observation.

But I saw Naples under circumstances the reverse of ordinary—at that critical period when it was the centre of interest to all the nations of Europe ; during the occurrence of events so strange and sudden that they resembled incidents of a romantic melodrama rather than real history. The achievements of Rollo and Robert Guiscard were repeated before the eyes of men who are never tired of saying that they live in a prosaic age. The interest of these events is scarcely abated, for they involve momentous consequences yet to come. The great captain who is now playing the part of Cincinnatus at

B

Caprera has potentially—like another captain who once enjoyed a temporary repose in the neighbouring Elba—an army at his command. He is one of the great powers, who, though not officially represented, makes his presence felt in all the councils of Europe.

I reached Naples two days before the departure of the King. What I saw and heard during the eventful three weeks which followed, will form the main part of my story. I prefer to tell this story (at the risk of occasional repetition) in the words of a journal written on the spot, and at the first leisure hour after the occurrences. In this journal I have corrected nothing but slips of the pen. I have inserted no *ex post facto* prophecies. I have merely added a note here and there by way of correction or explanation.

As the political interest of the time is my only justification for writing at all, I have cut out from my narrative almost all that had not relation to passing events. The excavations at Pompeii and the treasures of the Museo Borbonico have, for the present, lost their interest. Besides, there would be an incongruity in thus mixing contemporary history with antiquarianism and dilettantism ; nor would the space at my disposal allow me to do so, in any case. I might have touched in passing many such topics, and given conclusions without arguments ; but I remember the warning, " Brevis, esse laboro, obscurus fio," and I have reason to think that a love of brevity is liable to be mistaken for an affectation of smartness and a tendency to dogmatism.

I crossed from Folkestone to Boulogne in a storm of wind and rain., The rain accompanied me to Paris, scarcely abated during the two days of my stay there, chased me in flying showers to Macon ; then, withdrawing for a while, hung in masses of threatening cloud in front and flank as we crossed the plains and wound along the valleys, guarded with bastions of limestone crag on either hand, the first approaches to the great fortress of the Alps, to Culoz, now, alas ! a frontier place no more, thence by the lake of Bourget and Chambéry, where we saw skeletons of triumphal arches destined for the reception of the new master, to St. Jean de Maurienne, where we exchanged the railway for the diligence. The route of the Mont Cenis is, to my mind, the least picturesque of all the Alpine passes. But what it lacks in scenic beauty it makes up in historical interest, as being the route of Hannibal.* At Lanslebourg the clouds, which I had been comparing to hovering bodies of barbarians hanging on the line of the Carthaginians' march, burst upon us in a torrent of rain which lasted to Susa. When at length we reached Turin, at one A.M. (about thirty hours after leaving Paris), there was a cloudless sky overhead, and the soft sweet air of summer Italy to breathe and move in.

I had been much entertained by one of my companions in the banquette of the diligence—an Englishman going to join Garibaldi. Evidently a gentleman, he had "roughed it" through life with the strangest comrades. He had dug for gold in Australia, had driven an omnibus for six months in Melbourne, &c. &c., and now was about to seek his fortune in Italy. "Not," he said, "that he cared a button for one side or the other; he wanted if possible to get a commission in the Sardinian army, and meanwhile, at all events, to have a lark."

* This is conclusively established in a work entitled, " A Treatise on Hannibal's Passage of the Alps," by Robert Ellis, B.D. Fellow of St. John's College, Cambridge, 1853. The subsidiary arguments derived from the Peutingerian table, the names of places, &c., however ingenious and probable, are less convincing than the main arguments, and tend, on a first reading, rather to invalidate the conclusions. I am disposed to think that Mr. Ellis lays rather too much stress on the fact that the plains of Italy are visible from a point near the summit of the pass. Polybius, from his language, seems to suppose that the plains would be visible, as a matter of course, from the summit of any pass, and he himself probably crossed the Alps only once in the way of business ; and if he had such weather as has always been my fortune in crossing the Mont Cenis, he could not verify the fact. The story of Hannibal's encouraging his men by showing them Italy is, perhaps, after all only a rhetorical figment. Everybody not familiar with Alpine travel would take it for granted that Italy was visible from the summit (not having a clear understanding of the distinction between " peaks" and "passes"), and the situation, " Hannibal pointing out Italy to his soldiers," is too striking not to be accepted as true: " ut pueris placeat et declamatio fiat." I doubt, too, whether we have got at the true signification of λευκόπετρον. However this may be, Mr. Ellis seems to me to have proved his point abundantly.

I fancy that a good many of the volunteers, if they would confess it, were actuated by similar feelings.

I stayed nearly a week at Turin, where I found several old friends and acquaintances, several of them Neapolitan exiles, who gave me letters to their friends at home. Among them was Baron Charles Poerio, the gentlest and most innocent victim that was ever tortured by tyrant. I observed in him, as well as in others of his fellow-prisoners whom I saw at Naples afterwards, a subdued manner that was infinitely touching. It was as if long imprisonment had crushed their spirit and robbed life of its vitality. Poerio said that, during his short tenure of office, the king affected to treat him as a confidential friend, would offer him a cigar when he went for an audience, and so forth. On the anniversary of the day of his accepting office, he had the chains put on in the court of one of the prisons, the benevolent monarch looking on from a window.

I went one day to a charming villa on the "Collina," near Moncalieri, to visit an exile of a different race. I found him playing with his children, as youthful at heart as any of them. No prison had bowed his spirit down, and even eleven years of exile had not sickened his hope of triumphant return. He had not a shadow of doubt that the sword of Garibaldi would open through Venice a road to Hungary. "Shall we meet next year in London?" I said at parting. "We shall meet next year, if anywhere, at Pesth," was the reply.

On the 28th of August I went to Genoa, on the chance of finding a steamer for Livorno or Naples, there being no trustworthy information to be had in Turin. When I arrived there, I found that I had no choice but to wait till the 31st for the French boat. Three days soon passed among the varied sights of Genoa, the most beautiful as well as one of the busiest of the cities of the world. Garibaldi's portrait was in every window, ballad-singers were chanting his praises, and as you passed a group standing in the street or seated at the *café*, you were sure to hear the magic name. I was made all the more eager to get to Naples, fearing that he might get there before me.

I here insert some leaves of my journal, omitting, as I said, almost all that related merely to the regular "sights" on the way.

*Aug.* 23.—Turin is the most regularly built city in the world. It would have delighted an ancient Greek. Hippodamus himself might have planned it. Pausanias would have been in ecstasies if he had seen it, all its lines straight and all its angles right-angles. And in his' eyes the beauty of the regular city would have been enhanced by contrast with the rough shapeless mountains, glimpses of which you get at the end of the streets that run towards the north and west. Only the Contrada del Po deviates somewhat from the due direction, but this is scarcely appreciable by the eye. The spacious porticoes are thronged with people, notwithstanding that this is the season of the *Villegiatura*, and there is "nobody in town."

I went this morning to call upon a friend at the Ministry of Foreign Affairs, which is modestly lodged in a corner of the Piazza Castello. I was surprised with the quietness of the whole establishment. The porter was dozing at the door; my friend the *employé* was not at home, nobody was waiting for an audience, and M. de Cavour was "disengaged" in the inner room. "Did I want to see him?" asked the porter. Having no pretext for an interview with the great man, and having neither invention, nor impudence sufficient to extemporize one, I was obliged to decline the honour, and I went away wondering at the stillness which reigned at what may be called the central point of European diplomacy. It reminded me of the brain, which, though the source of all sensation, has no sensation itself.

*Aug.* 24.—This morning I had a call from Signor ——, a ministerial deputy, and an able as well as honest man. He takes a gloomy view of the state of things in Italy. "The

Ministry is excessively embarrassed by the exigencies of France, on the one hand; by the remonstrances of the great Powers, on the other; and by the popular enthusiasm for Garibaldi, on the third. (We may suppose an Executive to have *three* hands, at least: in this case all of them are tied.) Garibaldi is a brave man, but 'a fool' (*sic*); he is easily led by the people about him, and he is surrounded by the most worthless advisers—as, for example, Crespi. The Mazzini party are taking advantage of the discontent excited by the late measures of the Ministry against the volunteers, and of Garibaldi's easy temper, and hope to proclaim first the Dictatorship of Garibaldi, and then the Republic in Southern Italy. The ultra-liberals are blind to facts and consequences; they will not take account of the difficulties in their way; they menace Rome in spite of France and Venetia, in spite of Germany (for it is certain that Prussia has agreed to make common cause with Austria).

"Things are going from bad to worse, and we may lose all we have gained. Old animosities—*la politica di campanile* —are reviving again, and are fanned by the ultra-liberals for their own purposes. The people were humiliated at the loss of Savoy and Nice, but all reasonable men felt that the Government had no choice. The citizens of Turin cared much more for Savoy than Nice, because the change brought the French frontier within sight of their walls. Turin is now a defenceless frontier town, and can never be the capital of Italy."

*Aug. 25.*—I met another gentleman, neither deputy nor ministerial. He was enthusiastic for Garibaldi, "the honest man and great captain." "Cavour," he said, "has lost all his popularity, not so much from the cession of Savoy and Nice —for there was no resisting the armed brigand who took them—but from the way in which it was done. Cavour did it jauntily and unconcernedly, when, in decency, he ought to have worn an air of dejection. To parody what Jean Jacques said of a bishop: 'Quelque véridique qu'on soit, il faut bien mentir quelques fois quand on est diplomate;' but Cavour lied gratuitously. People have lost all confidence in him since he has sold himself to the devil.

"Garibaldi is true as steel; he will conquer Naples and proclaim the Ré Galantuomo King of Italy, who will then find some honester man than Cavour to be his prime minister."

*Aug 26.—Notes of a Conversation with* ——. "The franchise in Piedmont is given to all who pay forty francs per annum in direct taxes, which, in a country divided into small holdings, is almost equivalent to universal suffrage. But all landholders are conservative, and those of Piedmont Proper exercise it admirably; they are the mainstay of the constitution.

"The so-called Tuscan autonomy is not an autonomy in fact; the word is misapplied. It means in this case that, for the present, the judicial system of Tuscany is maintained intact. For instance, if a dispute arises in Tuscany, it cannot be tried at Turin till they send it for trial.

"Ten years ago, I foresaw that the idea of Italian unity was mounting like a flood, and would sweep all before it. The existence of this idea is a great fact which people at home would not see; I mean, secretaries of state. Naples might have been saved to the king, if he had joined Piedmont. In March, 1859, Lord Malmesbury wanted Sir James Hudson to go to Naples and advise the king to grant a constitution. He said, 'It is no use unless you allow me to advise his sending twenty thousand troops or so, to make a demonstration to the Italian side; a very small demonstration will suffice.' Lord Malmesbury refused; 'he did not wish Naples to be mixed up in the quarrel between Austria and France.' Now the quarrel between Austria and France was 'in the second plan.' The battle of Italian unity was uppermost in men's minds. The great Powers urged the Piedmontese Government to stop the departure of the volunteers as soon as Garibaldi turned his designs on the mainland. Legally, there is no distinction between Sicily and Naples, but morally there is a distinction, because the Sicilians had

been deluded by the Bourbons. The promise of a constitution, made in 1812, was never fulfilled. And, as you
remind me, Lord Palmerston said in parliament, apropos of
non-intervention, that there was no point of international law
which is not liable to exceptions in practice. Farini's cir-
cular was the result of this diplomatic pressure. If after
that he had not prevented the departure of the volunteers,
the power of Minister of the Interior would have been at an
end. He could not act otherwise than he did. The papers
cry out, but their influence is almost *nil,* since Parliament
has begun to perform its functions regularly. Ten years ago,
the press was very powerful. Cavour himself used to write
articles. Now each paper is the organ of some little knot
of politicians. Like a volcano (as you say) where there are at
first a number of little outlets which all cease when a great
crater is formed. If Garibaldi is beaten, the Piedmontese
Government will see that it must bide its time ; it will still
represent the idea of unity, which sooner or later will be realized
in fact. The more moderate papers are beginning to see the
necessity of waiting for an opportunity of getting Venetia.

" If Piedmont receives any further accession of territory,
there is a notion afloat that France will demand the island
of Sardinia as the price of her assent. The plains are
enormously fertile, yielding, they say, forty-fold. A large
outlay would be required for draining, &c. to bring land
now idle under cultivation. The volcanic rocks and the high
mountains which prevent a free current of wind from west
to east, are the cause of the unhealthiness of the place. All
the island is unhealthy part of the year, and part is unhealthy
all the year round. Sardinia is the most retrograde portion of
the kingdom, and disaffected because the high taxation has been
most felt there. There is an English party and a French
party eager for annexation to one or other country, which is
rich, and, as they think, would spend money there, but it
would not strengthen either. The Bay of La Maddalena
was of service to England in the former war, when they were
blockading Toulon ; but now that steam-vessels have taken

the place of sailing-vessels and can keep the sea in any wind, it will no longer be of service even in war. But politicians at home are governed by traditional views about British interests. That is why we stick to the Ionian Islands, which are no use to us. If we could only get rid of the notion that France is our natural enemy, and that we are bound to keep up posts of possible annoyance to her ! The Ionian Islands are a perpetual sore between England and Greece. With Malta it is different. It is an island-fortress—prize of war— and I am for keeping it as long as we can. It would be ridiculous at Malta, or Gibraltar, to submit the question of ownership to universal suffrage.

" The notion prevalent in Germany that the line of the Mincio, or at all events that of the Adige, is necessary to their security in a strategical point of view, is quite unfounded. It has not even the excuse of tradition. Read Metternich's letters, written at the time of the Congress of Vienna, and you will see that he was unwilling to accept the fatal gift of Northern Italy. But now that they have got the four fortresses, and that the Germans conceive their honour as well as their safety involved in the Austrian retention of Venetia, they will keep it as long as they can.

" After all, we must submit all questions at last to the inexorable logic of facts (as the French say). "

GENOA. *Aug.* 29.—Walked for an hour after sunset with a French gentleman, whose acquaintance I had made at dinner, up and down the delightful promenade of the Acqua Sola. It occupies an elevated platform on the eastern side of the city, flanked externally by the walls of the inner circle of fortification, and looking over a valley set thick with painted houses and gardens, the sea to the right, and on the left the hills crowned with fortresses. It is planted with rows of ilex, acacia and plane, and in the centre is an oval pond with a fountain, set round with weeping willows. It is well provided with stone seats. As we sat upon one of these, looking towards the sea, still lighted with reflected splendour from

the west—"It is a shame," said the Frenchman, "to talk
politics in so lovely a place, and at such a time. We ought
to talk poetry."

"It is your restless Emperor," said I, "who forces everybody to think and to talk politics at all places and times."

"Maybe so," he replied ; "but his view is the true view,
namely, that there will be no secure and lasting peace for
Europe until its political system is based upon the principle
of nationalities. It may cost us years of disturbance to establish this principle, but it will be the best for peace in the
long run. Europe will then be in a position of stable equi-
librium (as the mathematicians say). This is the object of
French policy. Surely it is nobler and wiser than the hand-
to-mouth purblind policy of your Government, which huddles
up all quarrels, and has for its object only the adjournment
of war in the interest of merchants and fundholders."

He spoke as volubly and rapidly as an actor in a Greek
comedy delivering the πνῖγος. When at last he paused for
breath, I interposed : "Stop ! what do you mean by 'the
principle of nationalities ?' "

"What do I mean ! Surely it is clear enough. It is a
phrase universally used. Everybody knows it."

"But if it has a definite meaning, it is capable of definition."

"Well, I suppose we may express it thus : Every nation
has a right to belong to itself, and to choose its own form of
government, and its own governors."

"What do you mean by a nation ?"

"Diable ! mon cher Monsieur, comme vous vous posez en
Socrate ! The words of which one knows the meaning best
are precisely those which one feels it most difficult to define.
Of such words no one asks for a definition in good faith, but
only for the sake of puzzling you, and in order to divert a
question of facts into a question of words."

"Don't be angry ! In all good faith, I do not know in
what sense you use the word 'nation.' Its etymology—"

"Oh, confound etymology—je m'en soucie guère. I use the

word in its modern sense, meaning a people of the same race, speaking the same language, inhabiting the same country."

" As for instance ?"

" The French, the English, the Italians—"

" Stay a moment. I doubt whether your instances are to the point. Are the people in Brittany, Lorraine, Alsace, and Gascony, of the same race as the people in the centre of France, and do they speak the same language ? Yet they are integral parts of the French nation. So it is with the Welsh, the Scotch Highlanders, the people in the Channel Islands— they are not of the same race, nor do they speak the same language as the bulk of the English nation, yet they belong to it, inseparably attached. Of Ireland I do not speak—"

" No, you would find a difficulty there."

" I may find a difficulty in combating the rooted preju- dices existing on the Continent with respect to Ireland, but you must admit—without prejudice to the future rights of King Macmahon—that it forms at present a part of the united kingdom, while two-thirds of the people are of Celtic blood : and a small portion still speak a Celtic tongue. As for Italy, it is inhabited by a multitude of races : Celts and Lombards in the north, Greeks in the south, and a fusion of old Italic tribes in the centre. As to language, a Lombard peasant and a Neapolitan peasant are as mutually unintelligible as an Englishman and a German."

" But there is one language for the educated classes. They understand each other."

" Yes, but that was not what you meant when you men- tioned ' a people of the same race speaking the same language.' Look at Hungary again. I suppose you would help in the establishment of a separate Hungarian nationality if you could ? "

" Oh, certainly."

" Well, in Hungary there are, I believe, at least four separate races, and four distinct languages, yet all these are united against the Austrian Government, and desire to form one independent nation. We read in the papers how cordially they fraternized at Pesth on the feast of St. Stephen, the other day."

" I admit, my definition will scarcely apply to actual facts; it is rather a definition of the beau ideal of a nation. Let me see if I can modify it so as to make it practical. You English can only comprehend what is practical. As the Emperor said, *you* will never go to war for an idea."

" For my part, I don't see that the annexation of Savoy is a whit more ideal than the annexation of Scinde, unless the combination of fraud with force in the case of Savoy—"

" Ah !" (with a prolonged sneer), " quant à la fraude un fils d'Albion a beau parler."

" Allons! let us not quarrel like a couple of commis-voyageurs, but revenons à nos moutons. By the way, where does that phrase come from ? Is it somewhere in Molière ?"

" No ; it is in the *Avocat-Patelin,* where you will find the source of a great many popular sayings." He mentioned several ; and, restored to good humour by this display of erudition, he said with a smile, "Ah oui, nos moutons; où en étions-nous ? "

" You were proposing, I said, to modify your definition of a nation. If you had stuck to it, I would have asked you further what you meant by 'race,' and then what you meant by 'language ;' and each of these words seems to me to be as difficult to define, practically, as 'nation' itself; that is to say, to lay down any rule capable of practical application as to what constitutes identity and what diversity in race and language."

" Well," said the Frenchman, "let us not quibble any more about words, let us come to things. I say then that a people, of whatever race or language, wishing to separate itself from, or join itself to, another people, has a right to do so."

" Pardon me, I don't wish to quibble about words ; but in using the term 'people,' you are in fact begging the question as much as if you had said 'nation.' "

" You are hard to satisfy. I will say, if you like, instead of 'a people,' 'a number of persons living together.' "

" Therefore, if the city of Bordeaux, for example, thinking its material interests more closely connected with England than with France, were to vote for annexing itself to the former country, the French Government would acquiesce ?"

" To say the truth, I don't think it would."

" That is to say, that when it found its interest opposed to its principle, it would follow its interest."

"No; your *reductio ad absurdum* is itself absurd. When I said 'a number of persons,' I meant, of course, such a number as might reasonably claim to form a separate nation."

" But in the case I put, it was not proposed that Bordeaux should form a separate nation."

" It would be ridiculous for Bordeaux to pretend to have a will of its own distinct from that of France, of which it forms perhaps in population the three-hundredth part. We punished, if you remember, a similar insolence on the part of Toulon."

" Yes, and you punished a similar insolence on the part of La Vendée, without any particular reference to the numbers of the revolted population."

"That was in time of war, and the necessity of self-preservation imperiously demanded the reconquest of Toulon and La Vendée."

" If you assist the Hungarians to revolt, will it not be 'time of war' then, and will not the necessity of self-preservation, from an Austrian point of view, demand the reconquest of Hungary ?"

" Have you then no sympathy with an oppressed people ? (You will permit me to use the word in this case.)   Do you not think that it is the duty of a great and free nation to protect the weak against the strong ?"

" Certainly, but then independent states, represented by their respective governments existing for the time being, have their rights.   These may be respected, and yet much good done in behalf of what you call oppressed nationalities, by peaceful diplomacy, friendly advice, grave remonstrance, or even formal protest.   I doubt whether the principles of

international law (which, I imagine, knows nothing of your
' nationalities '), would sanction a declaration of war in any
case."

"There are extreme cases in which necessity knows no law,
international or other. The state of Italy could not have
been remedied last year without war."

"I doubt that. In a general congress, Austria, by the
threat of war, might have been induced to erect Lombardo-
Venetia into an independent kingdom, with free institutions,
under the Archduke Maximilian, who was personally popular.
I believe that the state of Italy would have been better than
it is now. At all events a congress ought to have been
tried. France would have saved 50,000 men and 500,000,000
of francs, but then Louis Napoleon would have missed the
glory of commanding in a real battle, and Nice and Savoy
would have still belonged to Sardinia. When once you
unchain the demon of war, you know not where the end
will be. Over and over again peace has been made at
last without any reference to the original objects of the
war. No evils are comparable to those of war. The English
policy to adjourn war as long as possible, seems to me to
be the really noble and humane policy. Induce oppressive
governments to adopt gentler means of keeping public order,
and time may soften down the fiercest antipathies. Alsace
and Lorraine, which detested the yoke of France at first,
have now become French at heart; but if Germany had been
constantly inciting them to revolt by promises of military
support, successive insurrections would have been quenched
in blood, and mutual hatred perpetuated for centuries. The
policy of your Government towards other nations seems
to me the most mischievous possible ; it keeps up discontent
among the people, who are perpetually told how much they
are oppressed, and it piques the pride of the rulers, who will
not relax their system lest it should be said that they do
so from fear of France."

Surprised that I had not been interrupted during this long
speech, and receiving no reply when I paused of my own

accord, I turned towards my companion.  He was, or feigned to be, asleep.

*Aug.* 31.—I sailed from Genoa by one of the French steamers "making the scala," as the coasting voyage from Marseilles to Naples is termed.  There was a great crowd of passengers—the Neapolitan and Sardinian boats having been taken up for purposes of war.

Next morning we stopped at Leghorn, and the morning after at Civita Vecchia, and remained there six or seven hours, enough to enable a party of American gentlemen to pay their visit to Rome, by aid of the new railway.  They returned in triumph, having effected their purpose, and spent, as they said, "fifty minutes, sir, in the E-ternal City !"

A moist scirocco, the prevailing wind during last autumn, brought languor and discomfort to all.  We were right glad when about six next morning, September 2, we found ourselves sailing by Capo Miseno, and entering the Bay of Naples. Everything, however, was shrouded in a fog more worthy of England than of Italy.

As soon as we came to anchor, we were boarded by large parties of Neapolitans, chiefly in the new uniform of the National Guard, coming to meet their friends.

After a very cursory examination of passports and luggage, we drove off to the Hotel Vittoria, where I established myself for the next three weeks, in an upper room, looking over the ilex, acacias, palms, and pepper-trees of the Villa Reale.

I kept my eyes and ears open, went diligently wherever there was anything to be seen and heard; taking copious notes day by day, and occasionally writing long letters to friends in England.  The tomb of Virgil, Cumæ, Avernus, Pompeii, the statues and frescoes of the Museum, occupy a considerable space in my note-books.  All this I suppress for the reasons before mentioned.

*Extract of a Letter from Naples, dated Tuesday, Sept. 4.*

Naples is officially *in a state of siege;* practically, there is
no Government at all.  Every man does that which is right in
his own eyes, says what he pleases, writes and prints what he
pleases, and acts entirely irrespective of all law, military or
civil.  For instance, three officers of Garibaldi's army on their
way to England, charged with the duty of bringing out the
800 volunteers from Liverpool, landed this morning.  Their
passports bore no Neapolitan *visé*, so the police at the custom-
house refused them permission to enter the city, whereupon
they pushed the said police aside, and walked on in spite
of them.

A crowd of papers has sprung into existence during the
last few weeks.  They are all openly for Garibaldi.  They
record triumphantly the progress of the insurrection, and
exhort the citizens of Naples to be ready for action at the
right moment.  They are sold everywhere in the streets, and
as the price is generally one *grano* (something less than a
halfpenny sterling), everybody buys them.

At the theatres the audience demand " Garibaldi's hymn," a
patriotic composition, which is to the Italians of to-day what
" Yankee Doodle" and the " Marseillaise" were respectively
to the Americans and French in their time.  The hymn is
sung ; the audience stand up, join in the chorus, and, at the
conclusion, cry out tumultuously, " Viva Garibaldi," " Viva
Vittorio Emmanuele," " Viva l'Italia Unita."  I see portraits
of Garibaldi and of Victor Emmanuel in every shop ; I have
not seen one of Francesco II.

The universal opinion here is, that the reign of the Bourbons is over, and that Garibaldi will enter Naples without the
faintest show of resistance.  If the King had had, as was supposed, any party among his subjects, whether nobles or lazzaroni,* some manifestation would be made in his favour;

* *Lazzaroni.*  There is great doubt even among well-informed Neapolitans
as to the existence of an organized body to which this term is specially appro-

but there are no signs of the existence of a Royalist party. When the King drives out—as he did daily up to the end of last week— no notice is taken of him. Here and there a spectator, out of pity and courtesy, lifts his hat; but the majority ostentatiously keep theirs on.

Numbers of officers in uniform are driving about in hackney cabs, chatting and smoking, evidently in high spirits at the thought that they can turn their backs on the enemy as soon as he appears, and this time without dishonour. All accounts agree, that neither officers nor soldiers mean fighting. There is not one regiment upon whose fidelity the King can rely. There is one man in the army who is said to be faithful, viz. Bosco, who commanded at Melazzo : but Bosco is a Neapolitan. The National Guard, just organized, and very conspicuous in their uniform of blue coats and red caps, mount guard at various places in the city. They are to a man in favour of Garibaldi. I am informed, on good authority, that the King has given a promise in writing to the British Minister, and probably to all the foreign Ministers, that he will not in any case order his troops in Sant Elmo and the Castelli to bombard the city. A better security than the promise, written or otherwise, of a Bourbon, is the assurance that the troops would not obey such an order. The bombardment of Naples would not save the dynasty, and would eventually entail upon the bombarders certain destruction from popular vengeance. Wherever on the mainland the Neapolitan troops have encountered the Garibaldians, they have fired a few shots, for form's sake, and then surrendered. If such was their conduct when the ultimate result of the

---

priate. In general it is used vaguely to designate the poorest classes. A species of tax called "gamorra" is levied upon cabmen, small greengrocers, fishmongers, and other tradesmen, by the authority, and for the benefit, of a body of bravoes, called thence *gamorristi*, who co-opt into their body those who, by strength of arm and skill in the use of the stiletto, may have shown themselves worthy of the distinction. One of Garibaldi's earliest decrees declared this tax to be illegal. The account I have just given was told to me by a secretary of legation, long resident at Naples. This he believed to be the only organization among what are called "lazzaroni."

war was doubtful, how can we expect that they will act otherwise when the Bourbon cause is evidently desperate ?

If the 14,000 Swiss who served Ferdinand had been still here, they might have made a last stand for his son. Hated as they were by the people, their best security would have been a desperate defence ; but they are disbanded, and, as I before said, the unhappy Francesco has not a regiment upon which he can count. The very soldiers on guard at the gates of the palace seem to be under no discipline and no restraint. I saw them last night lounging in all attitudes, laughing, smoking, and playing at mora, with shouts that rang through the courts and must have reached the ears of the King.

As to where Garibaldi is, and when he may be expected here, perhaps you in England know as much as we know. All sorts of reports are circulated. The Café d'Europa is crowded all the evening with people circulating the bulletins issued every hour by this or that committee, and telling and hearing news the authenticity of which cannot be tested, and of which one half contradicts the other. " Garibaldi is at Vallo "—" Garibaldi is at Sorrento " —" Garibaldi is at Salerno " —" The King embarked last night "—" The King is going to-morrow "—" The King declares he will stay at Naples "— " The Ministry has resigned "—" The Ministry has fled in a body "—" The King wants to go, but the Ministry will not let him "—and so forth.

This much we know for certain, that the insurrection has spread from province to province and from town to town. Even Salerno * has established a Provisional Government and proclaimed Victor Emmanuel ; and Salerno is under the very eyes of the commander-in-chief of the royal army.

The least sanguine expect that, within a week at farthest, Victor Emmanuel will be proclaimed at Naples. Meanwhile, the city itself, with the exceptions I have mentioned, wears its ordinary aspect. Business goes on as usual ; all the shops are open, the streets are crowded with carts and carriages of all sorts. (By the way, Naples is the only Continental capital

* This anticipated the truth by two days.

which is liable to "blocks" such as occur in the thoroughfares of London.) Life and property are just as safe under the new police and the Guardia Nazionale as ever they were; indeed safer, because there are no *sbirri* to inform against honest men. Almost all the exiles have already returned without permission from Government, but certain that it dares not, and cannot, molest them. I have talked during the last two days with many persons of all ranks—I was about to say, of all opinions—but, in reality, I find only one opinion. All agree that the Bourbon rule is practically at an end—and the sooner it is nominally at an end also, the better. All look forward with joyful hope to the impending change, but there are some who fear that, between the fall of one Government and the installation of another, there may be an interval of anarchy, during which the lowest class may take an opportunity for acts of pillage and private vengeance. In case of this fear being realized, I am told that preparations are made for landing sailors and marines to guard the embassies and consulates, where, if necessary, strangers of the various nations may find refuge. But in this fear I do not share. Naples can never have a weaker Government than it has at this moment, when it is not governed at all; and yet, as I have said, the thieves and assassins are no busier than at ordinary times. In fact, the lazzaroni are a bugbear, which has long frightened the shopkeepers, and led them to suppose that a rigorous police was necessary to the protection of their goods and chattels. It is a generic term, including all the very ragged men and boys of the city—a class which, in times of revolution, may be terrible enough, but which is no more organized for mischief than the mob of London. The upper and middle classes, including in the latter class all labouring men with regular employment, are in this instance of one accord. Therefore I believe that the change of Government will be made without any disturbance and without any interruption in the ordinary business and social relations of the place.

In all likelihood, however, the conquest of Naples will

only be regarded by Garibaldi as a starting point for fresh enterprises much more uncertain and much more arduous. " The end is not yet."

*Sept.* 6.—After spending a long morning at Pompeii, I went with a young English officer by the train at one o'clock, towards Salerno.

As soon as the railroad turns away from the Bay of Naples, it traverses a valley which at the farther end narrows into a ravine. Castles crown each peak, towns and villages stretch in white lines along the slopes. The mountains are covered to the top with trees, ilex, elm, chestnut, the lower slopes with vines in festoons, olives, mulberries, maize yellowing to the harvest, cotton with pink and white blossoms, tomatoes golden among the green. At Nocera we saw the Neapolitan soldiers* in their light blue dresses, crowding the staircase and galleries of the great palace which serves for barracks.

There was a citizen of Salerno in the train, who made polite offers of his services there. We got to Vietri in about an hour, and taking a carriage, drove at a furious pace from that village to Salerno, perhaps two miles distant.

There we found the place all excitement. That morning a Provisional Government had been installed. Four officers of the national guard had taken the place of the Intendente nominated by the King. The Intendenza itself was decorated with Italian colours, and the arms of the Bourbon dynasty over the door were similarly concealed.

A few of Garibaldi's men in red shirts, the only article of dress which is *de rigueur*† in his army, were walking about the town. One of them told me that he had just received a telegraphic despatch, announcing that the general had left Eboli and would be at Salerno by six. Inquiring of another for General Türr, to whom I had an introduction, he took me

---

* They were part of the force which had just evacuated the lines in front of the capital, and were retreating to Capua—the fatal move which cost Francesco his crown.

† Even the red shirt, as I afterwards observed, was not indispensable. There was nothing *de rigueur* in that army.

into the Intendenza, and presented me to a white-haired, white bearded old gentleman, who, as I understood, was the general's secretary. He was very civil, but could not or would not give me any information.

We then strolled about the town, and went to the cathedral, which has an atrium in front, with columns and capitals taken from some Roman temple. There are a number of sarcophagi under the arches, which had been appropriated by Normans. You may see a knight in armour sculptured rudely, reposing above ; and on the side, a group of Cupids and Bacchantes. Two pulpits and the screen of the choir are beautifully preserved specimens of glass mosaic work, such as the tomb of Henry III. at Westminster, long ago defaced.* In the crypt below, rich in marbles, is the body of St. Matthew.

Returning to the beach, we passed one of the King's "Bavarians," very drunk, wearing a kind of cockade of the Italian colours, crying, as well as he could, "Viva Garibaldi," and supported by sympathizing natives. A bystander informed us with an air of triumph, that two hundred of these Bavarians had the previous night mutinied at Nocera, killed (*ammazato*) one of their generals, and one of their captains, and then fled in various directions, several having come to Salerno to offer their services to Garibaldi. This story was, we found, true in the main, only "the general" was an addition. They *had* murdered a captain. My companion, as a military man, took a very different view of the feat, which our Italian friends seemed to think meritorious on the whole.

As the day declined, the crowd gathered more thickly on the terrace which runs along the shore in front of Salerno. New detachments of tumultuary national guards poured in from the neighbourhood, armed with guns of all sorts and sizes, and without any pretence to uniformity in dress. A strong wind was blowing from the west, and clouds of dust

---

* Is it our damp climate, or our mischievous nature, which mutilates every monument in England ? The mosaics at Salerno look as if they had been wrought last year.

swept along the terrace, so that I thought if the General delayed his entry much longer, we should have no sight left to see him withal. The sun went down, and left the hills purple against the clear orange and rose of the sky.

Still he came not. By-and-by, men set out to meet him with bundles of torches ready for lighting, and the householders prepared to illuminate their windows. Bands of music paraded the town, and the crowd kept up a running fire of *vivas* to pass the time. At last, about half-past seven, a louder and more continuous cheer was heard; two or three carriages drove in, surrounded with people waving torches. It was he at last. As he stopped at the door of the Intendenza, the national guard closed in to keep off the crowd, and escorted him up the staircase. A few minutes after, he appeared at the balcony, while some one next him held a moderator lamp so as to throw the light full on his face. He stood bareheaded, fanning himself with his black wide-awake, and looking like anything but the daring freebooter that he is. He has the most benign expression of countenance, and his partial baldness and long beard give him even a venerable look. He might serve as model for the portrait of the most benevolent of ancient philosophers, whoever that may have been.* Long after he had retired, the crowd continued to cheer, "disturbedly," as the old stage direction says. In a little while all the town was lighted up. Nothing could be more beautiful than the lines of light spreading along the steep slopes of the hills and flashing in the sea below. By-and-by the moon rose, and touched with cold greenish light the rocky summits of the hills, convents, and castles, and white villas in the slope, bright enough to distinguish the grey rows of olives above from the thicket of lemon and fig trees below, and at last blending with the ruddy splendour that shone upon town and beach and sea.

We retired at last to sup and sleep at the Hotel Vittoria (almost the last house on the road to Vietri).

---

* The busts of Euripides, in the Vatican, have a striking resemblance to Garibaldi.

*Sept.* 7.—About half-past nine, we heard the roar of *vivas* in the street, and coming to the window, saw Garibaldi himself, passing in the direction of Vietri. One of the crowd, while cheering in the most frantic manner, suddenly fell in a kind of convulsive fit. I asked our landlady, a vivacious, black-eyed Calabrese damsel, whether he had not been *drinking* the General's health. "No," she said; "it is joy. Ah," in a tone of reproach, "you English, who have been always free, cannot imagine the delight of deliverance." And she made a gesture as if she were about to fly.

Beside Garibaldi sat a person with gold lace round his cape, who we were told was General de Suget, commander of the national guard. The question for us was, Whither were they bound? Our landlord assured us that they were going no farther than La Cava: he had it from the best authority—it was *certo, certissimo*. So we forthwith engaged a carriage to take us to La Cava. Just as we were setting off, came our acquaintance of the railway, in the uniform of a national guard, who told us that Garibaldi was going straight to Naples, and that we might still be in time to catch the special train that was to take him.

We drove with all speed to the station at Vietri, which was crowded with carriages outside and people inside. There was no chance of getting through in the regular way; so climbing up a somewhat steep bank, and getting over a low wall, we gained the railway. The train was not gone. Without asking any one's leave, we got into a third-class carriage, containing already about thirty people, like ourselves, a self-invited escort for the Dictator. We were welcomed with cries of "Viva l'Inghilterra." It seems that the Neapolitan authorities, after the departure of the King, had sent a telegraphic message to General Garibaldi, asking when and where it would be his pleasure to receive a deputation. The answer was: "Immediately, at Salerno." Accordingly, the deputation came early on Friday morning. To their question, when would the General honour Naples with his presence, he answered, "At once," saying that he preferred a spontaneous

to a prepared welcome. So every one was taken by surprise.
We congratulated ourselves upon our good luck in being there
to see. During the whole of our journey, the thirty or forty
occupants of the carriage where we were did not cease shouting and singing. Some were in the uniform of the national
guard, and almost all were armed in one way or other. The
most conspicuous figure was a priest on the podgy side of
forty, in the usual long black gown and broad-brimmed
hat, with a musket and wide tricolor scarf. His bass voice
was loudest of all in the choruses, and in the cheers as
we passed each successive station. In the intervals he was
smoking regalias, which he brandished with the left hand, as
he brandished the musket with the right. The songs were
interminable. Rather, as it was always the same tune and
the same chorus, I should call it one song of which the verses
were extemporized by one or other of the company. I
managed to remember two of these verses, which I give by
way of specimen.

> " Siamo Italiani,
> Giovani freschi,
> Contro ai Tedeschi,
> Vogliamo pugnar.

(*Chorus.*)     Viva l'Italia !
> Viva l'unione !
> Viva Garibaldi !
> E la libertà !

> Morte a Francesco,
> Del nome secondo,
> Piu belva nel mondo,
> Trovar non si può.

(*Chorus.*)     Viva l'Italia, &c.

The tune resembled the ordinary chant of the saints'
litany, " Sancte ——, ora pro nobis," *allegro* instead of
*adagio.*

At every station a mob of curious people were gathered,
who exchanged cheers with the occupants of the train, but
it was evident that they scarcely believed Garibaldi himself

to be present. Events had hastened to their *dénouement* so
rapidly, that people could hardly credit the evidence of their
senses. We stopped at Nocera, Torre dell' Annuziata, and
Portici, for a few minutes. The demonstrations of welcome
came from all classes; from the fishermen who left their
boats on the beach, from the swarthy fellows, naked to the
waist, who were winnowing their corn on the flat house-roofs,
as well as from the national guards who crowded round the
carriage to see the famous chief.

At Naples there was a little delay while the Minister of
the Interior, who has transferred his services directly to
the Dictator, made a complimentary speech, not a word of
which was audible to us. Then Garibaldi got into the
carriage which was waiting for him, and drove slowly by
the Strada Nuova, the Strada di Porto, and the Largo del
Castel Nuovo to the Foresteria. A few carriages followed
containing the deputation, and perhaps a dozen of his officers
in their red shirts. He himself wore his ordinary costume,
red shirt, black wide-awake, black neckcloth, and a coloured
silk handkerchief knotted and hanging down his back, to
serve, I suppose, on occasion for protection against the sun.
A detachment of national guards went before and behind.
We elbowed our way among the shouting crowd, and kept
close by his carriage all the time. The excitement and enthusiasm were great, but the crowd was an extemporary crowd,
composed of persons who had suddenly left their work at the
news. Naples had been taken by surprise. The windows
were not filled with expectant faces, the houses were not decorated with flags, because no one knew that he was coming.
This robbed the event of its beauty as a spectacle, but it threw
no doubt on the heartiness of the welcome.

Garibaldi sat for the most part apparently unmoved, but
from time to time he lifted his hat, and smiled, as it were,
with the eyes rather than the lips. One of his men, with red
shirt and plaid scarf and plumed hat, well armed, stood behind
the carriage at his back, keeping, as I thought, a sharp eye
upon all who came near, as if looking for the handle of a

dagger, or the butt end of a pistol.   As we passed the Castel del Carmine, a number of the King's troops, still in garrison there, were looking on.   The mob in passing called to them, and, with menacing gestures, demanded that they should cry, "Viva Garibaldi."   Some few obeyed, but the majority stood with folded arms and closed lips, notwithstanding the imprecations of the crowd below.   The procession at last reached the great open place (its shape forbids me to call it a square), in front of the palace.   Then Garibaldi left his carriage and entered the Foresteria, a large house intended for the reception of foreign guests of distinction.   A few minutes afterwards he appeared at an open window on the first floor, and walked along the balcony to the centre of the building.   Loud cries, not like the rolling cheers of an English crowd, but confused and inarticulate, greeted his appearance.   He leaned with his left arm on the iron framework of the balcony, and waited patiently hat in hand.   At last the crowd began to understand that he wanted to speak to them, and gradually the cries and shouts died away into silence, obedient to reiterated "Zitti, zitti," from the quieter spirits.   It was to the following effect :—

"You have a right to exult in this day, which is the commencement of a new epoch not only for you but for all Italy, of which Naples forms the fairest portion.   It is, indeed, a glorious day and a holy—that on which a people passes from the yoke of servitude to the rank of a free nation.   I thank you for this welcome, not only for myself individually, but in the name of all Italy, which your aid will render free and united."*

He spoke with a clear and loud voice, which was heard by all.   The phrase " Italia intiera " occurred twice in his speech, and was pronounced with unusual distinctness and emphasis, eliciting cheers of especial meaning.

Wearied with dust, heat, and excitement, I went home to bathe and rest, and found that some patriot had picked my pocket.

* No newspaper, that I saw, contained a perfectly accurate report of this speech.

Meanwhile the Dictator went to the cathedral, where a service of some kind was performed, and thence to the Palazzo d'Angri, where he has taken up his abode for the present.

About three o'clock I drove up the Toledo, and found the street in front of the Palazzo blocked up by a dense mass of carriages and people on foot, crying "Viva Garibaldi !" at the top of their voices, to bring him to the window. At last one of his men appeared and laid his cheek upon his hand, implying that the general had gone to lie down—"his custom always of an afternoon" (as I am told). He gets up about three in the morning and transacts a vast amount of business before the rest of the world is out of bed. Before the day was over, every house, almost every window in the Toledo and Chiaia and main streets of Naples had its flag. There seemed to be considerable difference of opinion as to what the Italian tricolor was. All were agreed as to the colours, green, white, red ; but whether they should be placed like the French, parallel to the staff, or like the Dutch, at right angles; and whether the green should come first, or the red, seemed to be a moot point which each householder decided according to his fancy. The white portion of the flag was adorned either with a portrait of Garibaldi, or with a red shield and the white cross of Savoy. At sunset the town was illuminated, as the Italians say, *à giorno;* crowds of pedestrians and a multitude of carriages paraded the main streets. The noise was indescribable. The hero's name was repeated in all manner of forms, as if it was a declinable noun—Garibaldi, Garibaldo, Garibalda—nay, it was metamorphosed into Gallibar and Gallipot, and Galliboard; at last the two first syllables were suppressed, and " Viva *'Board* " was the favourite cry, the sound of the last syllable being prolonged to the utmost. You heard too, " Viva Vittorio Emmanuele," and still more frequently, "Viva l'Italia unita," which at length was shortened into *una,* and when people got so hoarse that they could not articulate any longer, they held out the forefinger and shook it as they passed, indicative of their desire for unity. Men,

women, and boys, crowded the carriages and clung to them
like swarming bees—I counted thirteen persons in a small
vehicle drawn by one horse. Some waved flags, some
brandished daggers, holding them occasionally in unpleasant
proximity to one's throat, and shrieking with menacing
scowls, "Viva Garibaldi!" others danced frantically along,
waving torches over their heads. I have never seen such
a sight as the Strada di Toledo presented as you looked up
it, the long lines of stationary lights converging in the
distance, and the flags drooping from the windows, and down
below the mad movements of the torches, and the waved
banners and gleaming arms. Here and there an excited
orator addressed the crowd about him in wild declamation;
little bands of enthusiasts, headed sometimes by a priest and
sometimes by a woman, went dancing through the streets and
burst into the *cafés*, compelling all present to join in the
popular cry. I was forcibly reminded of the scenes of the
French Revolution and Mademoiselle Louise Theroigne. When
I was in the Café d'Europa a priest rushed in with frantic
gestures, with eyes starting from his head, with a banner in
one hand and a knife in the other, uttering horrible and
inarticulate howlings. Having seen him, I can understand
the frenzy of the ancient Bacchantes.

A friend of mine saw a young and beautiful girl, belonging
apparently to the upper class, who, standing up in a carriage,
began to address the crowd quietly at first, but warming
gradually into a fury of enthusiasm, the veins in face and
neck swollen, and ending with "Morte ai Borboni," shrieked
out with the accents and gestures of a Rachel.

*Sept.* 8.—The diversion was repeated on this night (and
again on Sunday, the 9th), with more vigour and violence
and extravagance than ever.

An unfortunate man who did not cry "Viva Garibaldi"
when he was bidden, was ripped open by one who carried
a dagger, and died on the spot. An English officer saw
him lying dead. A proclamation next morning from the
new minister of police entreated the people to leave their

arms at home, but it did not appear to have much effect.
These people have not been accustomed to official en-
treaties.

On the afternoon, Garibaldi went to the Church of the
Piedigrotta, seeing (as the paper informed us) that it had
been the ancient custom of the Neapolitan Sovereigns to pay
their devotions to the Madonna of that ilk on the 8th of
September.

There used to be a great parade of troops on this day, and
country people came in from far and near ; but this year it
had lost all its usual characteristics.   There were no troops
and few visitors, and a heavy fall of rain completed the
failure.   This I heard from others, as I spent the day at
Puzzuoli Cumæ and Baiæ.   I returned in time for the performance at the San Carlo, which the Dictator was present at.
The performance was listened to with impatience ; people
seemed to care for nothing but shouting "Viva" between the
acts.   Some English midshipmen, from boxes in the third
tier, made themselves very conspicuous, by the energy with
which they waved their tricolor.   The spectacle was spoilt
by the avarice of the managers, who had doubled the prices
and consequently halved the audience.   The thousand or
fifteen hundred who were present did their best to com-
pensate for the beggarly account of empty boxes.   "Viva
Venezia" seemed to be the favourite cry.   I saw the Dictator
smile grimly when he heard it.   Among the persons who
came to pay their respects to him was, as I was told, the
very Admiral who had commanded the Neapolitan fleet at
Palermo, and also Liborio Romano, who bowed in the
humblest manner, " con illimitato rispetto."

The ballet was brought to an untimely end by some one in
a shooting-coat rushing on the stage and crying out, "Viva,"
&c. in which the whole *corps de ballet* joined, crowding round
the box where the General was and lifting their arms in
the theatrical fashion of supplication.   A body of national
guards, with drawn swords, escorted Garibaldi through the
thronged corridors to his carriage.   Some one, in loud voice,

cried "Silenzio nel nome de Garibaldi!" which was answered
by a prolonged shout.

*Sept.* 9.—About ten o'clock, as I was walking by Sta.
Lucia, I saw a great crowd gathered round a brightly blazing
pile—a curious sight on a summer's morning. Asking a bystander the meaning of it, I was informed that the pile consisted of the furniture, books, and papers of an obnoxious
agent of police. He was about to make his escape. Some
of the mob being informed of it were on the watch, and as
soon as the cart containing his chattels emerged from the
door of the fortified place where he lived, they pounced upon
it, made a heap of its contents, and set fire to them. They
were dancing round the fire in wild excitement. Old women
threw up their skinny arms and shrieked, and the children
were mad with delight. I saw one man seize a loose sheet of
manuscript, which had been blown away from the pile,
crumple it in his hand, throw it down, and stamp on it, then
fold his arms and "stare with his foot on the prey," in the
attitude of Clytemnestra stamping on the corpse of Agamem-
non. The Neapolitans, generally speaking, are not handsome
in feature nor picturesque in dress—they are common-place
when in repose, but when excited with passion their countenances and gestures are a study for an actor or a painter.
While they were thus engaged, a rumour spread that the
owner of the furniture was making his escape by sea. In-
stantly the crowd dispersed. Some put off in boats, others
clambered round the rocky point and along the sea-wall—all
animated with a desire of vengeance. They were, however,
disappointed. The obnoxious functionary either was already
gone, or else he prudently waited for a more favourable opportunity.

It is probably because the officials of the King have been
for the most part as prudent as their master, and made their
escape in time, that so few acts of violence have been com-
mitted during these revolutionary days. It is not for want of
will on the part of the people. To-day I read in the paper

that as Garibaldi was returning from a drive, some one followed him, crying, "Viva Francesco II.," when a "Guardiano della Dogana" came up and shot him dead ! The mob wanted to inflict indignities on the corpse (as their wont is), but the Dictator interfered, and ordered that it should be decently buried. It does not appear that he blamed the slayer for excess of zeal.

This afternoon I saw at the Castel Nuovo the King's troops with bag and baggage and arms evacuating the place, and the national guards marching in. A considerable crowd assembled, but there was no manifestation of feeling against the soldiers. About 150 of them waited for an hour or more in the street outside. Passers-by talked to them in friendly terms. As far as I could judge from the countenances of the men, they were quite indifferent, and did not seem to care where they went. They were well armed and clothed, and evidently had been well fed. Had they been well led too, things would have taken a very different turn. While they were still waiting for orders, a regiment of Garibaldians came by, marching, it was said, under General Türr, to repress a reactionary movement at Ariano. The contrast which these filibusters presented to the royal troops was exceedingly striking. Of the Garibaldians, no two men were armed or clothed alike : some had only one shoe, some no shoes at all ; there were boys of twelve and thirteen years old in the ranks, side by side with grey-bearded veterans ; there were the most *bizarre* contrasts as to personal stature, such as one has only seen in the army of Bombastes Furioso, and they made no pretence of keeping line or keeping step. Many of them carried loaves stuck on the end of their muskets or bayonets. Yet these are the men before whom a well-appointed army of 150,000 men, with a king's name for a tower of strength, have broken, and fled, and melted into nothing.

Apropos of the boys, I was told by one who had seen the battle of Melazzo, that they did excellent service, and showed no sign of fear—laughing and singing, when exposed to a murderous fire, as if their young lives were of no account.

"If such things be done in the green tree," the kingdom of Italy may in reality be formidable to her neighbours a few years hence, and justify the alarm which led Louis Napoleon to appropriate Nice and Savoy for the protection of France.

*Sept.* 11.—Now that the shouting is over, we have some leisure for thinking what it means, what realities lie under this surface of triumph.

On Wednesday night, Sept. 5th, or rather, early in the morning of Thursday, the King left his palace, committing the town to the care of the general commanding the national guard. The official paper, *Constitutional Journal*, as it was called, contained on Thursday a proclamation from the King in dignified terms, promising that when it should please the Divine Justice to restore him to his throne, he would still preserve the constitution which he had granted. To this was added a protest, countersigned by the prime minister De Martino, in which Garibaldi is called "un ardito condottiere."

The same journal of Friday, changing the title of constitutional to that of official, and substituting Naples for the Two Sicilies, contains a proclamation of Garibaldi to the people, dated that morning at Salerno, and a letter from Liborio Romano to "the most invincible Dictator," announcing the impatience of Naples for the arrival of its "Redeemer," and professing "to await his further orders with unbounded respect." This man had two days before countersigned the deeds of Francis the Second in his capacity of Minister of the Interior. His ostentatious treason has offended even the Neapolitans.

The mode in which the title now borne by Garibaldi was conferred, is singular. Some half-dozen persons, including Liborio, announced that on the invitation of the General they had formed themselves into a provisional Government, and in virtue of the authority so derived they declared General Garibaldi dictator. A curious *ruse* this for investing the transaction with a semblance of legality. It can only impose upon those who do not see that arguing in a circle proves nothing. By what authority, we may ask, did Garibaldi invite the said half-dozen to form a provisional Government?

The gazettes of Saturday and the two following days are filled with decrees nominating ministers, confirming all subordinate *employés*, except pluralists, in their posts, recognising the national debt, &c.

The ministers named are not in general (as I am told) men of commanding ability, but they are all moderate men, and, as such, give satisfaction to the party represented by the Comitato Unitario, the Cavour party.   The party which calls itself the Partito d'Azione, of which Crespi, De Pretis and Bertani (perhaps I should now include Mazzini) are the leaders, is, however, believed to have the Dictator's affections, and in reality to guide his councils.   Garibaldi has already alarmed the moderates by the violence of his language more than once.   On Friday, in answer to an address, he called Lamoricière " a renegade head of a set of ragamuffins without country and without faith."

The King of Sardinia (I am told) sent an aide-de-camp to consult about the mode of annexation, to which he replied, " It is not even to be thought of till I get to Rome ;" and this story is confirmed by the proclamation of this morning, September 11th, to the Sicilians, in which he declares his intention of proclaiming Italian unity from the summit of the Quirinal. This audacious boast has dismayed the moderate party exceedingly.   In a constitutional *régime* the ministers would all have resigned.

In the midst of all these political agitations I have found time to visit many of the permanent " sights " of Naples, and especially the Museo Borbonico, which, like the British, contains several museums in one.   The picture gallery may, I suppose, be ranked as the sixth in combined excellence and size, after those of the Louvre, Dresden, Madrid, and the two at Florence.   It has not so many great pictures as the Vatican, or even perhaps our National Gallery, but they are small galleries.   In sculpture, it ranks next to the Vatican and before the Louvre ; in ancient bronzes and mosaics it is *facile princeps ;* in ancient frescoes it is unique. The frescoes, taken all from Herculaneum and Pompeii, are exceedingly interesting.    In point of art, their quality is very various. Some figures are drawn and coloured with a breadth and boldness that reminds one of the Venetian school.    There is, for example, a brown stalwart Bacchante which Titian might have painted.    But in general they recall the style of the earlier naturalists of Florence more than any other modern school The " house-sign-and-ornamental painters " of a country town in the first century had attained a mastery over pencil and brush which, till Masaccio came, the greatest artists of modern times failed to equal.    But then the devotional feeling, the divine calm that charms us in Giotto and Fra Beato, is altogether wanting.    Their conceptions are of the earth, earthy.    I suppose, however, that we should have found this devotional element in the works of the best painters contemporary with Phidias.    He, at least, believed in the gods he moulded, Zeus and Athene.

In these frescoes, even when the drawing is bad, the conception is often good, and now and then we meet with a dash of humour, which, coming to us from a long-buried world, is infinitely charming.    The idea we derive from our schooldays of the old Romans is that of a grim, savage, earnest people, who were always fighting, marching, sacrificing, making military roads, innumerable laws, and interminable orations, growing by-and-by foully and desperately wicked Nothing brings us so near to them as a glimpse of their capacity for fun such as we get in the dramatists now and then, in Cicero's letters, or in Suetonius, or in these frescoes from Pompeii.    For instance, there is a series of small pictures (absurdly described in the catalogue as signs of shops) representing fat winged Cupids hard at work at various trades.    In one they are making boots, very like the modern " Bluchers." I cannot tell why they are comical, but I defy any one to look at them without laughing—which I take to be the best proof that they are comical.

In the centre of the room is a recent addition, quite the reverse of comical—a wax mask found in a tomb at Cumæ along with a headless skeleton, from which it is inferred that the person interred had been decapitated. It is, I believe, the only relic of the kind in existence. The chances are immensely against the preservation of so fragile an object. In the tomb were found some coins of Diocletian. A few years ago the remains would have been at once assumed to be those of a Christian martyr, and a new saint added to the calendar.

I have been to-day, Sept. 12th, with a party of English and Italians to visit the prisons of Naples, in virtue of an order given by I know not what minister. First we saw some dungeons at the Prefecture of Police, behind the Largo del Castello—places without light or air, or bed or seat, where we were assured people were kept for a fortnight, or even a month, without trial. One of these, built for a common latrina, had been used, as one of the new officials told us, for a prison, and a man was confined for eight days there, at the end of which time his toes were found to be gnawed to the bone by rats. The sight and smell of the place made two of our party ill for the whole day.

Then we went, by steep, narrow, filthy bye-streets, to Sta. Maria Apparente. There the cells had been newly cleansed and whitewashed, so that there was nothing disgusting in their appearance; but the prison system in vogue under Ferdinand was such as to convert the most spacious and airy room into a place of torture. There is also a winding passage cut in the rock, which seems formerly to have been divided into cells. Several unfortunates had carved their names, with the date of their imprisonment. One recorded that he had been buried (*sepolto*) for four years, 1856—1860; another added to his name the words, " Reo senza delitto."

After that we climbed up to Sant Elmo, saw its vast subterranean galleries tier above tier, with sloping staircase (if that may be so called which has no steps), like the passages in the Mausoleum of Hadrian. There are prisons also in St.

Elmo, though they have been chiefly used to punish military offenders.* We walked round the ramparts, now sentinelled by Piedmontese troops and by the national guard, and soon, it is said, to be demolished. As a fortress, St. Elmo is formidable to the town, but of little use against an enemy from without, at all events, if he approached by land, as it is completely commanded by the hill on which the Camaldoli stands.

If we may trust the story told us by the officer who was in command of the fortress, the gunners wished to bombard the town on Sunday, and when their officers refused, they shut them up in a guard-room, all but the commandant, who, as he informed us, pretended to be with them in feeling in order to prevent their design. According to his account, he, with the aid of a few soldiers, got a gun in such a position as to command the mutineers, who, not being able to point the guns themselves, at last desisted from their purpose, and went away to their homes or elsewhere. So the officer in question retains his command under the Dictator. When I told this story to an eminent Garibaldian colonel, he said that he did not believe a word of it. The story is, indeed, palpably inconsistent. Why should sixty gunners (for that was their number) not be able to point a gun without their officers? and how could he get a gun to bear upon all the soldiers within the fortress? Fancy a man, wearing epaulettes and a sword, telling such a lie with unblushing face!

* A long account of what we saw that day in the prisons was given in a letter published in the *Times* early in October, by Lord Llanover, who was one of the party. The facts there stated are, of course, strictly correct, but I hesitate to accept some of the inferences drawn or implied. We must remember that the prison at the Prefecture of Police, far the foulest of all, had been recently devoted to the purpose for which it was originally intended, and we had no proof beyond the word of an *employé* of a few days' standing that it had ever been used for a prison at all. And in the other cases our informants were all men who had just been appointed to their offices by the new Government, who knew nothing of the former system of their own knowledge, but were anxious to blacken the late reign, and could not fail to see that each atrocious detail communicated a thrill of sensation, rather agreeable than otherwise, to their auditors. We have evidence enough, from more trustworthy sources, of the cruelties practised by Ferdinand. But I do not think there is any proof that the prison system at Naples under Francesco II. was at all worse than it was in England under George the Third.

*Sept.* 13.—The same party which had visited the prisons of Naples went to that of Ischia in a despatch-boat, commanded by Captain Marryatt, a son of the novelist, and kindly placed at our disposal by Admiral Mundy. On our landing we were assailed by a crowd of natives offering donkeys and figs, three donkeys at least to each man, and more figs than one could eat in a month, clamouring in all tones from howls of exultation to whines of distress, till the poor stranger became so bewildered that he did not know whether he was expected to mount the figs and eat the donkeys or *vice versâ.*

The prison we were to see is in the Castle of Ischia, which Stanfield's picture has made familiar to English eyes. Only as we saw it the sea was rippling quietly about the base of the breakwater in the foreground, not tumbling in wild billows over it.

Some difficulty was made about our admission; but the combined authority and eloquence of Lord Ll—— and Mr. Edwin J——, aided by the fact that we had come in a ship of war, triumphed over all obstacles.

The prisons here were tenanted only by fleas. They were not particularly dark or dirty, or in any way horrible. We asked in vain for the torture-chamber and the thumb-screws, and on the whole could not but feel disappointed at the result of our inquiry. We were shown the room where Poerio was confined during some of his ten years of durance. There were four rooms *en suite* so arranged that an inspector could look on from a window in his chamber above, and see what was doing in any of them. The wooden tressels on which the prisoners slept and some fragments of their clothing still remained. They had the liberty of walking in a small walled courtyard.

The Ischian prisons were under the charge of the same keepers as before, old soldiers chiefly, who were very much alarmed at our visit and our questions, and as anxious to dissemble the rigours of the former Government as the new keepers of the Neapolitan prisons had been to exaggerate them.

*Sept.* 15.—I went by railway to Castellamare, and thence, with a carriage, in an hour and a quarter to Sorrento. The Neapolitan coachmen drive like Jehu the son of Nimshi. Even when one takes them by the hour they scarcely abate their ordinary pace, which is very different from the snail-like motion of a London or Paris cabman under similar conditions. One of Dr. Johnson's immortal truths was communicated to Mr. Boswell in these words: "Sir, there is something very exhilarating in the rapid motion of a post-chaise;" and I fancy that the Neapolitan driver feels the pleasure so intensely that he cannot forego it for the sake of sparing his cattle or spinning out the time, even when to him time is money.

The drive to Sorrento is one of the most beautiful in the world. The road at first follows the coast-line, winding into each cove and rounding each headland, then strikes across the valley where Vico is situated, crossing the gorge by a noble viaduct, doubles the next promontory, and, by a gradual descent, comes to the comparatively level plain of Sorrento. This plain is composed of a *couche* of tufa perhaps three hundred feet deep at the base of the hills, and sloping gently down to the water's edge, where it breaks away in an abrupt precipice, varying from one hundred to one hundred and fifty feet in height. This tufa has been deposited in the hollows of the limestone hills by some pre-historic volcano. It has been cut into deep gorges by mountain torrents many ages ago by slow degrees, for the channel is not sensibly deeper than it was two thousand years since, as may be seen by the substructions of Roman bridges, cellars, &c. still apparent. The plain is of wonderful fertility, and, except where there is a street, a house, or a lane sunk between high walls, it is like a continuous garden, "a contiguity of shade," fruit trees of all kinds oranges, lemons, figs, pomegranates, and trellised vines, where you may walk under a roof of matted leaves and pendent clusters. On the amphitheatre of hills which shelters the plain on east, south, and west, you see terrace above terrace, partly artificial and partly the natural formation of the white limestone rock, sprinkled with grey olives, relieved by the

brighter green of carob-tree, or fig, or vine, up to the foot of
the steep crag, or the verge of the native forest.

No wonder that the Romans were fond of such a place.
The beauty of Baiæ must have been in great part artificial,
even before its neighbourhood was altered and spoiled by the
eruptions of the Solfatara and the Monte Nuovo, and now it
presents a somewhat bare hill-side cumbered with shapeless
ruins. Baiæ, too, must always have been much hotter than
Sorrento, for the former looks towards the south-east, the
latter due north.* When the poet said, "Nullus in orbe sinus
Baiis prælucet amœnis," he meant an especial stress to be laid
on "amœnis," and referred not to the natural beauty only, but
to the society and various artificial *agrémens* of the place.
If people ever read Statius now-a-days, they would find that
even among the Romans there were some who preferred
Sorrento. Perhaps the eruption of Vesuvius in '79, which
half-suffocated the people at Baiæ, but so far as we know did
not affect Surrentum, may have contributed to establish the
latter in popular favour. Certain it is, that the ground there
was so valuable they they built villas below the cliff on
foundations laid in the sea itself. Large blocks of lava in a
regular line may be seen below the water from the Hotel della
Sirena, and to reach the shore you descend through galleries
still covered with stucco, and showing traces of colour. The
face of the rock is filled with artificial niches and caves,
evidently belonging to Roman houses. On either side of the
city is a deep ravine, offering at every step the most lovely
combinations of tufa rock and ruins and luxuriant creepers.
Round the city is a mediæval wall of great strength once, but
now crumbling and ruinous. In the centre is the Cathedral,
an ancient church with an open atrium like that of Salerno,
but thoroughly modernized. Outside there are some columns

---

* The modern Sorrentines maintain the superiority of their town to Naples
in amenity and healthiness. They have a couplet, the produce of a native
genius, which they quote with as much pride as if he had succeeded in making
it rhyme :—

"Napoli bella, Sorrento civile ;
Chi venga ammalato a Sorrento si sana."

of costly marble fitted with capitals not originally belonging
to them, the spoils probably of one or more ancient temples.
Near the Cathedral is a remarkable loggia, open on two sides,
like the Portico of Orcagna, only on a smaller scale. The
arches are round, and the capitals are carved in the flat
manner characteristic of Italian Gothic. It is called the
" Settina dei cavalieri," but I was not fortunate enough to
find any one who could give me an intelligible account of
its destination.

I rode in the afternoon of Saturday to the Deserto, a
convent now abandoned, and situated on the crest of a hill
south-west of Sorrento, commanding a view of the bay of
Salerno as well as the bay of Naples. The place was
tenanted only by a peasant (a " colon " they call him, still
retaining the Latin word,) and his family. The cells were
fast going to ruin, and so was the wall which had inclosed
round the convent an irregular space of perhaps a hundred
acres. Though the wind was "proprio scirocco," there was
a delicious coolness about it as I stood on the convent roof.
My guide, a good-humoured and in his way intelligent fellow,
had been employed with others by the Count of Syracuse
to excavate an ancient cemetery close by, which, from his
mention of the gold ornaments and other relics found, I
suppose may have been the burying-place of Theorica, a
Greek city, supposed to have occupied the site of the neighbouring village of Torca.

" This campo santo," said my guide, " was two centuries
(due secoli) old; before the world."

" Before the world ?" I asked. " How could that be ? "

" I mean," he said, " before *this* world; in the time of
another world, which was destroyed by a deluge."

" And that," I asked, " was two secoli ago ?"

" Precisamente, eccelenza."

" And how many years are there in a secolo ? "

" A hundred, or thereabouts."

" Well," said I, with the air of an inquirer thirsting for
information, " what happened about the deluge ? "

" The flood was sent, eccelenza, because the world was full of bad people ; but there was a signore called Noë, who was good. Dunque," he proceeded, putting his finger alongside of his nose, as their manner is when coming to the point of a story, " Jesus Christ, made a great ship, and put Noë in it ;" and so he went on with the narrative.

I have given the man's exact words. I tell the incident, as it seems to me characteristic of the amount of education of an ordinary Neapolitan of that class. There is no point in the story except this—that it is a fact.

I have always noticed that genuine tradition has a tendency to diminish the interval of time which has elapsed since the event of which it preserves the memory. I remember asking a farmer, who lived on the field of battle near Nördlingen, whether he had ever heard of such a battle. " O ! yes," he said, " he had often heard his father speak of it, and *his* father, who had seen it, told *him*." The remotest event is always supposed to be " in my grandfather's time." This is characteristic of genuine tradition. Forgery, on the other hand, has a tendency to magnify a nation's antiquity, and may sometimes be detected and distinguished by this mark.

*Sept.* 16.—I learn that, last night, a commissary of police, accompanied by some gens d'armes, arrested the Archbishop of Sorrento and carried him off to Naples. He had been the King's tutor, and so, I suppose, was suspected very naturally of favouring the Royal cause. He is much respected, they say, by the people, and is a good man. Surely it is a mistake for a Government which has just proclaimed liberty to tread in the steps of the old tyranny. What harm could an aged priest do if left alone ?

Though the Palermitan monks, and Father Gavazzi, and a few priests have declared loudly for Garibaldi, and though some have even joined the Neapolitan volunteers, the great majority are evidently for the King. The spirit of Garibaldi's movement is thoroughly anti-Papal.

Attempts are being made by the clergy to enlist the superstitious feelings of the people in favour of the King. It was reported that, on the day of the King's departure, the Virgin of Santa Lucia wept tears of blood. The church was crowded with persons who went to see next day. My informant saw the streaks which the tears had left. Last Sunday, too, I have heard vaguely that a friar preaching somewhere appealed suddenly to an image in the church, and asked whose emissary Garibaldi was, and the' image answered distinctly "Satan's."

We shall see whether Saint Januarius's displeasure will be shown in the non-liquefaction of the blood next Wednesday. And in that case, will Garibaldi adopt the plan of the French general in command at Naples, who threatened to shoot the officiating minister unless the miracle were immediately performed ?

*Sept.* 17.—In company with an English friend, I took a boat from Sorrento to Capri. A steady scirocco carried us in an hour and a half to the entrance of the Blue Grotto, where a smaller boat from the little port of Capri met us. In this we entered the low mouth of the cave with some difficulty, as there was a swell rolling in. One has a natural aversion to hackneyed sights which you are bound to see because "everybody" sees them, and I went to this grotto prepared to find it unworthy of its fame ; but I was compelled to admit the contrary. It is like a scene of enchantment, or the dream of some Eastern tale-teller—a cave with a floor of liquid turquoise and a roof of frosted silver. How is it that the same effect is not repeated in other instances? There are caves enough in other shores. How is it that Capri alone is favoured with two exhibiting this wonderful appearance, and why is one a "blue" and the other a "green" grotto ?

The colour of the sea outside the cave was a mixture of dark purple and indigo—such a colour as I have only seen when a strong wind was blowing ; and the sky was rather veiled than clouded—as is the case generally during a scirocco. We remembered the οινοπα ποντον, "the wine-like sea" of

Homer, but it is not likely that the familiar epithet which is as frequently applied to the sea as "swift-footed" is to Achilles, should have been suggested by a rare and exceptional phenomenon. The phrase probably came down to Homer from earlier and ruder poets, who would observe nature as the author of "Chevy Chase" observed it, but would not scrutinize it like Wordsworth. They saw that gold was red, and woods were green, and they needed no other epithet even for variety's sake. I believe that $οινοψ$ simply meant coloured, like wine, as distinguished from the bright transparent water of a fountain ($αγλαον$), and from the dark black water of a well ($μελαν$). In this sense, the epithet is always applicable to the sea, whether it be calm or troubled, whether it be blue, or green or purple.

We landed at Marina, a little village lining the beach at the only point where there *is* a beach. Elsewhere a wall of steep rock rises abruptly from the sea. We rode on donkeys through the vineyards and olive-grounds, to the little town of Capri, perched along a ridge, and thence up to what are supposed to be the remains of one of Tiberius' villas. It was a festival at Capri, so we saw all the *belles* of the island, plump brunettes, with dark eyes and hair, tight-laced black bodices, and white muslin handkerchiefs thrown over their shoulders. Capri is famous, we were told, for the industry and morality of its inhabitants, which, we will hope, is the reason why so many of our countrymen have chosen this island for the site of their hermitage.

Or does the gloomy spirit of Tiberius still dwell there as the *genius loci*, attracting kindred spirits? Lest this should offend any one, let me hasten to say that I do not consider the stories told by Suetonius and even Tacitus as worthy of belief. Court scandal is the most easily invented of all scandals, it is the most readily credited, and the most difficult of disproof. The memoirs of hangers-on about a Court are always to be received with suspicion, be they even written by a Duc de Saint Simon, or a Lord Hervey, much more when they are written by some nameless lackey who has no honour to tarnish, and is therefore quite irresponsible for his statements. Suetonius and Tacitus probably derived their Court gossip from a similar source, for it is very rarely that they give authority for their assertions. They only reject a story when it is palpably inconsistent with some other story they have heard. When two memoir-writers had told the same tale, they accept it and endorse it without a suspicion that both may be lying. The medals which are supposed to confirm the worst charges against Tiberius are found, to the disgrace of the ancient world, at many other places besides Capri. The story told by Suetonius about Tiberius throwing criminals down from a precipitous rock for his amusement, is probably a fiction. But it is likely enough that the tremendous precipice shown as the Salto di Tiberio (or Timperio, as the Capriotes call him) may have been in Suetonius' mind when he repeated or made the tale. The peculiarity just alluded to in the Capriote dialect reminded me of a cognate fact—that the modern Greeks express the sound of b by m and p. For instance, they spell tobacco, "tampakko."

One bourgeois, a Corsican, has opened a little restaurant at the Salto di Tiberio. He has bad wine, worse water, and makes exorbitant charges. I am sorry to say this of an old soldier decorated with the St. Helena medal. He has put up an announcement at the Marina in the following terms (I give it *literatim et punctuatim*) :

"Avis au Salto Tiberio onna ovver un restaurant de ce lo calon guii de la vue du golfe de Salerno et Pesto." *

*Apropos*, I noticed at Pompeii a jocular recommendation of the Hôtel de Diomède, printed by the landlord, beginning, "Je ne suis pas ce terrible Diomède qui faisait tant de peur aux Troyens et Cæsar." The "et Cæsar" is admirable. A name at which the world grew pale is always good for rounding a sentence.

---

* The interpretation is this :—" Avis : au Salto de Tiberio on a ouvert un restaurant. De ce local on jouit de la vue," &c.

*Extract of a Letter, dated Naples, Sept.* 18*th.*

Naples has passed from the government of the King to that
of the Dictator with more ease and with less disturbance of
public order than any one could have anticipated.  Business
has not been suspended for a single day, and, but for the
noisy demonstrations of delight which continued for three
days after the entry of Garibaldi, a stranger might have lived
in Naples without knowing that there had been a change of
masters.  The newspapers will have given you fully detailed
accounts of Garibaldi's facile conquest, and of the tumultuous
joy with which it was hailed at Naples.  I have been through-
out an amused and interested looker-on; but I need not tell
a tale with which you are already familiar.  I will merely
mention summarily the successive events in order to add a
touch here and there from personal observation.  Up to the
last moment there were some who believed that the King
would not abandon Naples without a struggle.  On the afternoon of Wednesday, Sept. 5, it was known that his troops
had received orders to fall back from Salerno, and it was
supposed that they would occupy La Cava and Nocera, and
defend a pass which is so well calculated for defence.  But
later in the day we heard that they were abandoning all
their positions in front of Naples, and were marching by
way of Nola to Capua.  It was obvious that the King had
given up the game for lost, and that he himself must follow
his troops and abandon his capital.  All that night there was
an unusual stir about the Palace ; every window was lighted,
and hurrying shadows flitted past within ; crowds waited
round the gates in the vain hope of seeing the departure of
the Court, their motive being, as I gathered, not loyalty, but
curiosity.  Carts loaded with furniture passed out from time
to time, the property, I suppose, of Goldsticks, and Chamber-
lains, and Lords-in-waiting.  " The rats are leaving," said one
of the crowd.  A Council of Ministers was held in the Palace,

which did not separate (it is said) till three in the morning. They were engaged in "redacting" the two proclamations which appeared in the Gazette of next day, in the second of which, countersigned by D. Martino, Garibaldi was called "un ardito condottiere." At the breaking up of the Council, the King went on board ship for Gaeta, the Ministers dispersed to their homes, except Liborio Romano, who hastened to offer his services to the Dictator. The conduct of this Romano is universally condemned. While Minister of the King he was in correspondence with Garibaldi, and, instead of defending the interests of the Crown, he did all in his power to thwart them. He wrote, immediately after the retirement of the Sovereign, a letter to Garibaldi, couched in the most fulsome and abject language. A man must be *morbo proditor* to be proud of his treason, as Romano seems to be. On Thursday, September 6th, I went to Salerno, saw Garibaldi's entry there, and returned with him to Naples. In some respects his reception at Salerno was more striking than that at Naples. The people of Salerno had been expecting him for some hours, and had had time to make preparations , the people of Naples were taken by surprise, and the crowds that gathered hastily all along the line of his passage through the city were evidently half-incredulous, and doubted whether it were he or not. There were no flags on the houses. This was all Garibaldi's doing, who said he preferred a spontaneous welcome. The square in front of the Foresteria, from a balcony of which he addressed the people, was not a quarter full. The demonstrations, however, on that and the two following nights were the most noisy and tumultuous scenes that I have ever witnessed. As far as I could judge, the makers of the noise, in very few instances, belonged to the lower classes. The shriekers, the spouters, the torch-bearers, the wavers of flags, and the brandishers of daggers, were persons from the well-fed, well-dressed orders. The lazzaroni are, I believe, quite passive and indifferent ; the priests and peasantry Royalist—but the priests are naturally timid, and the peasantry only feel keenly on a question of cheap bread and cheap fruit.   A Masaniello must appeal to this sentiment to have success either with peasants or lazzaroni.

The process by which a show of decency and order was given to Garibaldi's nomination as Dictator was curious. First half-a-dozen individuals, with Romano among them, constituted themselves a Provisional Government on the invitation of the Dictator of Sicily, and then, by virtue of their authority as Provisional Government, they nominated him Dictator of the *Two* Sicilies.   His first acts gave satisfaction. He chose his Ministers from the Moderate party—the party (that is) which follows the inspirations of Cavour.   And for a few days " all was for the best, under the best of all possible " dictatorships.   But latterly, the acts and words of the Dictator have given great alarm.   In his proclamation to the people of Palermo he spoke of the miserable men who counselled immediate annexation, and declared that he would proclaim Italian unity on the top of the Quirinal.   Then, in an order of the day *apropos* of the death of De Flotte, he alluded sarcastically to the Government of Louis Napoleon.   Finally, in a letter to one Brusco, he contradicted a rumour that he had been reconciled to Cavour, and said that he could never be friends with " men who had humiliated the national dignity and sold an Italian province "—which seemed even to include Victor Emmanuel.   People here are aghast at his imprudence. They ask themselves, Is this a game which he is playing with the secret connivance of the French Emperor, whose heart is with Italy, though he is obliged, as the eldest son of the Church, to keep up a show of opposition ?   Or is the Emperor bribing Garibaldi's counsellors to urge him on a path that must lead to his ruin ?   Is Victor Emmanuel consulted, and, if so, does he approve ?

The telegraph is, of course, interrupted at Gaeta, and we only heard, yesterday, of Victor Emmanuel's entry into the Roman provinces.   Is this step taken in conjunction with Garibaldi, or is it intended to anticipate and in a measure thwart him ?   These questions may be answered before you receive this letter.   At present, every one seems lost in un-

certainty. I have spoken of the Moderate party, which
includes, I suppose, the vast majority of educated men above
twenty-five years old. The other party—the party of action
—consists of Bertani, Crespi, and, of course, Mazzini, and
boys in general. The latter party seems to have lost its head
in the intoxication of success. They talk of marching to
Rome as one talks of taking a drive along the Chiaia. Father
Gavazzi * is the prophet of the party. His somewhat common-
place declamation has had great success. He preaches every
alternate evening in the square of San Francesco di Paola.
To hear democracy lauded in the front of a Bourbon palace is
a fact sufficiently piquant to give a zest to the most ordinary
oratory, just as the mildest jest becomes irresistibly comical
in church.

Several other decrees of the Dictator have given great dis-
satisfaction, as, for instance, that appointing Alexander Dumas †
Director of the National Museum, and commissioning him to
prepare a great work on the antiquities of Naples and the
neighbourhood. The Neapolitans are justly indignant at
having a vagabond foreigner, of abandoned character and no
knowledge of antiquities or of art, set over the heads of so
many persons infinitely his superiors.

The Dictator's weakness is said to be his submission to
favourites. Any one may lead him by the nose, if he
takes hold the right way. Bertani is, according to the
"Moderates," his evil genius. Meanwhile, with the growing
discontent of the Moderates, we hear from time to time of
reactionary movements at Avellino, and other places. Forty
peasants were brought in yesterday, tied together with

---

* A mistake. I heard the Father once afterwards, and read other discourses,
printed from shorthand writers' notes. He always counsels moderation, and
disbelieves in unity without monarchy.

† The pranks of this man, while dressed in his brief authority, were
incredible. I saw him one night parading Naples in fantastic costume,
attended by a score of men waving flags. At each station of the National
Guard they stopped, formed a ring round Dumas, and cheered.

He wrote to Admiral Mundy requesting arms and ammunition for his body
guard, and when his letter was returned to him by way of answer, he applied
to the French Admiral, whose reply was as decided, and still less flattering.

ropes—a sight of ill omen for the new Government. On Saturday, the Archbishop of Sorrento, the King's tutor, was arrested, and brought to Naples. Last night, there was a general alarm and anticipation of reactionary movement among the lazzaroni in Naples itself. The national guard was under arms all night, but nothing happened. My impression is, that things are getting rapidly worse, both here and in Sicily, and that Garibaldi will not be able much longer to govern the country. The sooner the annexation takes place and a regular Government established, the better for all parties.

*Sept.* 18.—I went with Mr. D—— to Sta. Maria Maggiore, at present the head-quarters of the revolutionary army. Finding that we were too late for the ten o'clock train, we engaged a large-wheeled single-horse vehicle, something like the now extinct English taxed cart, and in little more than two hours reached Sta. Maria. The road passes through Aversa, and lies for the most part over a perfectly flat and exuberantly fertile country, called *par excellence* Terra di Lavoro, for every yard is under cultivation. On the way, we fell in with a party of Neapolitan soldiers wearing their side-arms. They were making their way across country to join the royal troops at Capua, or where best they could. We had some difficulty in finding our way into Sta. Maria, owing to the barricades which defended the entrance of the principal streets. Happening to ask some question of a portly gentleman whom we saw in the street, he volunteered to show us over the town, escorted us to the amphitheatre, and offered us the shelter of his house, which he said was not magnificent, but entirely at our disposal, such as it was. The last offer we declined for want of time, but it was made in all sincerity. This is one instance of many within my experience of the especial favour with which we English are regarded at the present time by the Liberal party. Our new friend gave us to understand that he was one of the principal legal functionaries of the place, whether as judge or advocate we did not know, and the frequent respectful greetings that he received attested the truth of his pretension. He was an ardent Garibaldian, and anti-Papal to the uttermost. As a boy, he had been educated by the Jesuits at the Collegio Romano, but the oppression under which he had suffered with his countrymen had completely effaced the lessons of the fathers, and had inclined the tree in the opposite direction to that in which the twig had been bent. He told us that Ferdinand, who lived hard by at Caserta, regarded Sta. Maria with peculiar aversion, and kept it under police regulations of extra strictness. He used to say, " Whenever I go through Sta. Maria, I tread on republican stones." The employment of Lamoricière's mercenaries by the Pope had alienated, as our friend said, the firmest of his Holiness's friends. Italy was now virtually a Protestant country.

The amphitheatre is still a magnificent ruin. The two walls which formed the outermost corridors of the ellipse were unluckily built of hewn stone, decorated with marble columns at the entrance. These, therefore, were pulled down to furnish materials for the palace at Caserta, and probably also for earlier buildings. The brick and rubble work remains nearly intact. The amphitheatre of Capua, when entire, was, except the Coliseum, the largest of all. It served as a model for that of Puteoli. The subterranean constructions are on the same plan. The chambers and passages were lighted by a large longitudinal opening along the major axis of the ellipse, and by square openings all round. At the time of the exhibitions, of course, beams were laid over them, and the whole area strewn with a thick covering of sand. One may see the places where the beams rested. The vast space underground did not serve merely, as we are told in the guide-books, for prisons of criminals and dens of wild beasts, but it was the residence of the gladiators. There are plenty of conduits, wells, and drains for carrying off the rain water, so as to keep the place always dry and habitable. The stone seats for spectators have shared the fate of the outer walls, and been carried off. I observed, that in some of the corridors arches of brickwork had been added subsequently to the erection of the building, in order to strengthen the supports of the cavea.

Returning to the town, we took leave of our volunteer cicerone, and went to pay a visit to the General commanding in the absence of Garibaldi, Hieper, or Eber, as his name is variously spelt. I had been acquainted with him when discharging a more peaceful mission at Constantinople some years ago. The palazzo to which we were directed is a charming residence, with large lofty rooms painted somewhat in the Pompeian style, and polished floors deliciously cool, with a garden of lemon and orange-trees behind.

First came a ruddy-bearded aide-de-camp to ask our business. I begged him to aver la bontà, &c. &c.

"Sprechen Sie Deutsch, mein Herr?" he said.

I answered in the affirmative, and said that I supposed he was a Hungarian, like the General.

No, he was "Echt Deutsch aus dem grossherzogthum Baden."

There were many Germans, he told us, in the army, even Bavarians and Austrians, who looked forward to making " *ein* Deutschland," after they had made *Italia una*. Meanwhile they must, I should think, have to exercise all their proverbial national patience, hearing, as they do, perpetually repeated cries of " Morte ai Tedeschi!" We found the General suffering from a fever caught in the marshes of Cosenza, and scarcely able to walk. However, the politeness of a true gentleman never fails. He got up from the sofa, and gave us a kind welcome, though he must have wished us at—the headquarters of Francesco II. He gave us a written permission to visit the outposts, of which we availed ourselves at once.

In the streets at intervals we found bodies of the Garibaldians with piled arms, sitting or lying on heaps of straw strewn on the shady side ; some sleeping, some smoking, some mending their clothes, some cheapening figs—(although, without cheapening, you get for a halfpenny as many as one could eat in a day), all apparently in high spirits and good health, more like "jolly beggars" than a regular army. A

barricade of boughs is placed across the brick arch of Roman
work which formed the gate of old Capua, and is on the road
to the new—distant about two miles.  Half a mile beyond is
the line of infantry sentries, who stand at irregular intervals,
from fifty to one hundred yards apart.  They take their work
easily, leaning against a vine-clad poplar in any attitude they
may fancy.  Provided they do their work, Garibaldi and his
officers do not seem to care how they do it.  A martinet
would be sorely out of place here.  A quarter of a mile farther in advance, four poplar trees have been felled, and lie
across the road.  In front of them is a sentry on horseback.
We asked him if we could see the Neapolitan outposts.  " O
yes," he said, " come along with me, and I'll show you them.
When we go forward, they always come out to look at us."
When we had gone about a hundred yards, they did come out
accordingly, two on horseback and four on foot, about a
quarter of a mile off.  Having satisfied our curiosity, we
returned, in obedience to the advice of the General, who had
warned us not to go too far, as they were in the habit of
picking up stragglers.  What earthly good it would have done
them to pick us up, I cannot conceive.  If they had taken a
fancy to pick us *off*, it would not have been so pleasant.

Our expedition terminated without the shadow of an ad-
venture, but it was interesting as the only glimpse I had ever
had of a state of war.  Evidently it is not in Garibaldi's army
that one must look for " pride, pomp, and circumstance."

We returned by railway.  As we passed the splendid Palace
of Caserta, we saw the great square in front filled with troops.
They are under the command of General Türr.  At night, I
am told, they sleep inside and outside of the palace, as they
best may.

This is the result of Ferdinand's policy.  His army is
scattered, and revolutionary soldiers occupy every corner of
his favourite abode.  It is reported that he had no misgivings
and no remorse, and that almost his last words were that
" he died with the consciousness of having done his duty."
He sowed the wind, and his son has reaped the whirlwind.

*Sept.* 19.—I have just returned from San Gennaro, where I have witnessed the far-famed miracle. I went about half-past eight and found the Cathedral partially filled, and a dense crowd in and about the chapel of San Gennaro—a spacious octagon on the south side of the nave. National guards were keeping the door. At a quarter before nine, a loud shout rose from the crowd within. It was a greeting to the saint, whose image in silver gilt had just been placed on the altar. The shout was renewed as the priest adjusted the mitre and cope with which the image was clothed, and again, as an attendant lighted candle after candle beside it. An aged priest, standing within the altar rails, then raised aloft the vessel containing the sacred blood, and at once a forest of waving arms rose above the crowd, and the building rang with frenzied exclamations. Some other priests and assistants now appeared in the organ loft ready to lead the *Te Deum* whenever the miracle should be achieved ; meanwhile, the old man continued to hand round the vessel to let all the bystanders see that there was no deception, that the blood was really solid. The vessel in question is a kind of monstrance, round, with glass on each side, and two handles, one above, one below. It is more like a carriage-lamp than anything else I can think of. Inside, are two small phials containing an opaque substance, the blood of the saint. In order to show that it was solid, the priest turned the monstrance upside down, holding a lighted candle behind it, and showed it, round to the spectators just as a conjuror does before commencing his performance. All this time the crowd kept shrieking and screaming —the old women especially were frantic in their cries and gestures, moaning, and sobbing, and stretching out hands in nervous tension. Some men even were affected with this hysterical passion, and wept and moaned like the women. The confusion of endlessly reiterated prayers, uttered in such tones that they resembled imprecations, reminded me of the chorus of the priests of Baal in the *Elijah;* only here the trebles preponderate over the basses. Mendelssohn may have witnessed some such scene; but, so far as I know, the like is only to be seen at Naples, and in the Church of the Holy Sepulchre at Jerusalem on Easter Sunday. For any other parallel, one must go among fetish-worshipping savages.

The priest then turned his back on the audience, and the agitation of the crowd reached a point where it could no longer be expressed in articulate cries, for nothing was heard but sobs and groans. A very few minutes had elapsed, when the priest suddenly turned round and exhibited the blood LIQUID! A wild howl of exultation rose up; flowers were thrown towards the saint, and, strange to say, a number of birds let loose,* which the spectators had brought with them for the purpose. Never had the miracle been performed so soon. All were agreed on this, and eager discussions were going on in all parts of the church as to the exact time it had taken. Was it three minutes or four, or four minutes and a half? The old women were wild with joy. It was clear that San Gennaro was in the best of tempers towards his dear clients, and not at all displeased with them for turning out their king. Two of Garibaldi's red-shirted soldiers, who were making their way out of the chapel, were the objects of tenderly affectionate demonstrations; old women held up their hands to bless them, others patted them on the back and smiled approvingly. As soon as the shout that greeted the miracle had ceased, the men in the organ loft began the *Te Deum*, and the spectators joined in fervent chorus. Above the din we heard the guns of all the forts thundering out their joy. (There must be some means of telegraphic communication with the forts, as very few minutes elapsed before the cannon was heard.) By-and-by the sacred vessel was carried to the high altar, and successive bodies of worshippers were admitted within a railed space to kneel and kiss it, having first assured

---

* This, I afterwards learned, is the custom at all the great festivals of the Church, and symbolizes the soul's joy when delivered from the sins and sorrows of earth. It is a literal rendering of that passage in the Psalms, " My soul is escaped as a bird out of the snare of the fowler. The snare is broken, and we are delivered."

themselves by means of the candle that the liquefaction had
taken place. Some of the crowd near us were very anxious
that we should do the like. "Make way," they said, "for the
English Signori. Sergeant," to the officer of the national
guard who was keeping the wicket, "admit the English
Signori." But we declined the honour, and waited till the
priest—the same who had officiated in the chapel—brought
it round. As there was no candle placed behind it for our
benefit, and as the outer glass was dimmed with the kisses it
had received, we were not able to ascertain the fact of the
liquefaction. But all who have seen it before and after with
the aid of the light, agree that the blood, if blood it be, is
certainly solid first and liquid afterwards. There is no
deception so far. But admitting that, I cannot but remember
that I have seen the Wizard of the North and Wiljalba
Frikell do as much, and more, with their enchantments. It
is certain that the belief of the crowd in the chapel was
genuine and profound. This crowd consisted of persons of
all ranks, though the poorer classes preponderated. It would
scarcely have been prudent for Garibaldi, in presence of this
intense and deeply-seated superstition, to forbid the miracle as
the *Times* hoped he would. An *émeute* might have been the
consequence.

"Paris vaut bien une messe," said Henri Quatre. Garibaldi may say, "Naples vaut bien un miracle."

Some days ago I was expressing to a Neapolitan my wish
to see the liquefaction. "Do not mention it," he said; "it fills
me with shame." I cannot doubt that this is the general
feeling of most educated men, but it is not universal, for
among the weepers and the kissers to-day I saw several who,
from their dress and bearing, certainly ought to belong to that
class. One young priest, of rather attractive countenance, came
out of the chapel, his eyes red and his cheeks swollen with
weeping, but most of his order seemed impassive and did not
attempt even to counterfeit devotion. The venerable old man
in rose-coloured robes, who officiated, showed no feeling whatever. Probably perfect self-possession, with a little manual

dexterity, is the quality most requisite in the officiating minister.*

*Sept.* 19.—This evening our dinner was enlivened by animated accounts of a battle which had taken place in the morning, and at which half a dozen of the guests of the hotel had had the luck to be present. They had to tell of hairbreadth escapes, exemplary coolness under first fire, the cowardice of the Garibaldian troops, and their own courage. England had nearly lost an eminent barrister and an eminent artist by a grape-shot, which carried away part of their carriage, a third had arrested the flight of a regiment with his umbrella, a fourth had parried a cannon-ball with his walking-stick.

The real facts, as far as I have been able to gather them by subsequent inquiries, are these : General Hieper and Colonel Roskow, commanding the centre and left, had orders to make a feigned attack upon Capua, while Garibaldi and Türr were to cross the Volturno a few miles up the river and cut off a body of the enemy, occupying a plain on the other bank. Roskow, however, mistaking his instructions, attempted a real attack. As soon as he advanced into an open space in front of the gate of Capua, and within reach of the artillery having no artillery himself, his men were cut down by the fire from the bastions, and refused to advance. As soon as a body of royal cavalry showed itself, they fled precipitately, the officers being the first to set the example. Such was the panic that they rushed through Sta. Maria, and did not stop till they had passed the town, and saw at last that there was no man pursuing. One of my informants saw with his own eyes two of Garibaldi's officers crouching under a haystack to strip off their red shirts, lest they should be recognised. A more disgraceful panic was never seen. The good folks of Sta. Maria, that republican city, made haste to take all the tricolor flags from their windows. Even that which floated

* The secret is known only to the priests of San Gennaro and Mr. R. Monckton Milnes, who tells me that he has not merely witnessed, but once performed the miracle.

from the windows of the house which was General Hieper's head-quarters disappeared.   The national guards stripped off their uniforms, and all was prepared for the return of his Majesty.   Had the royal army had a leader, they might have marched to Naples unopposed.   Meanwhile, Hieper had nothing to do, and did it.   Türr and Garibaldi, on the right wing, found their road barred by a fire of artillery which they could not face, and finally retreated to Caserta.   The number of killed and wounded in the revolutionary army amounts, according to the best informed statements, to about one hundred and fifty.

The varying accounts of this engagement illustrate the propensity of Italians in general, and Neapolitans in particular, to invention and credulity combined.   The *Lampo* for instance, a Garibaldian organ, had the audacity to affirm that the royalist losses amounted to eight thousand in killed and wounded, whereas they could not, by the nature of the case, have exceeded twenty or thirty.   But invention is not confined to the Neapolitans.   On the authority of one of Garibaldi's generals, it was asserted that the possession of Chaiazzo was the object which the General had in view in making his attack, and that that object had been attained.   Military men not connected with either party affirmed that it would be impossible to hold Chaiazzo, being a position quite isolated on the other side of the river, and that no one would have thought of making such an attempt.   Up to the day I left Naples, September 22d, it was a matter of doubt whether it had really been taken or not.   The last news I heard before leaving was that it been retaken by the royal troops ; but it was doubted whether this, too, was not an invention to cover the other lie, and account for the fact that it was in the possession of the Garibaldians no longer.

One lives at Naples in an atmosphere charged with falsehood, and it is impossible to get a breath of native truth.   From the evidence of independent witnesses, it is certain that the Garibaldians met with a severe check, the moral effect of which has been very great, and more than counterbalances the manifestation of San Gennaro's favour in the morning.

*Sept.* 20.—Hearing that it was probable the battle would be renewed this morning, I went, in company with Colonel B—— (who had seen the engagement of the previous day), an English officer, and another friend, to Sta. Maria, whence, finding all tranquil, we proceeded to St. Angelo, a village about three miles off, above which is a hill commanding a wide view of the scene of war. Leaving our carriage at the village, we climbed through oak coppice to the sharp edge of the hill. In ascending, we had a good bird's-eye view of the plain of Capua, and of some 2,500 cavalry occupying it. From the ridge we looked over the winding Volturnus, on the farther bank of which is another plain, divided by a low range of hills from that of Capua, and also occupied by the royal troops. There were two regiments of cavalry and three or four of infantry ; double sentries, at short intervals, lining the bank of the river. We were so near that we heard the words of command, and, occasionally, one man calling to another. As we were some time examining them with our glasses, we at last attracted their attention, and a little knot of men gathered on the bank and fired about twenty shots at us, without hitting or coming near us. A tremendous thunderstorm, which had been threatening for some time and at last broke, was much more effectual in dislodging us from our position. We crept behind an overhanging rock, hoping that the rain would cease. From our lair, looking south, we had a prospect of bare, peaked hills, with castles on the top, and agreed, that if we had been transported there in sleep, we should, on waking, have thought ourselves in Rhine-land. But close round us were growing shrubs that never clothe the bleak northern hills—dwarf ilex, and myrtle, and the judas tree. As we descended we were caught in a still more violent shower, and took refuge in the crater of an extinct lime-kiln, where we found a dozen or more peasants and Garibaldini already housed. One was a captain of artillery, who gave us rum and tobacco, and in the course of half an hour communicated, unasked, the story of his life. He told us of his innamorata, showed us her picture and handwriting, and said that he had joined Garibaldi that he might have an opportunity of doing some heroic deed, and might say on his return to the lady of his love (here he threw open his arms), "Ecco-mi! son degno di te!"

*Sept.* 21.—On going out after breakfast, instead of being assailed by half a dozen cabmen shouting in my ears, cracking their whips in my eyes, and driving across my path, the wheels just missing my toes, I found the stand deserted. It was the same at another stand. There was not a cab to be had. On inquiry, I found that the Government had pressed such carriages, public and private, as they could lay hold off, and sent them to Santa Maria for the conveyance of wounded men. The other cabmen had made off directly, and hid themselves and their horses. Everybody inferred that a great battle was expected, so I immediately walked off to the railway station, where I arrived just as the train was starting. (At these times a ticket is a needless formality—quite an unnecessary expense. You are never asked for your ticket, nor expected to pay anything except a small gratuity to the official who gets you a seat. It is an ill wind that blows nobody good. Even a time of war has its advantages.) When I reached Santa Maria, I found that I had again come on a false alarm. The carriages had been impressed to bring back to Caserta those who had been wounded on the previous Wednesday—such of them, that is, as were capable of removal. I went to see those who remained in one of the hospitals at Santa Maria. The wards were tolerably clean and airy, and the wants of the poor sufferers seemed as well attended to as circumstances permitted; but it was a sad sight. In one case the ball had entered the eye and gone out in the neck—a terrible wound; but the surgeon said he had hopes of saving the man's life. In another case the ball had carried away part of the lower jaw and all the teeth. The saddest case of all was that of a poor child of ten years old, who, with his father, was driving a cart on the day of the battle. They were compelled to come into the field to help in moving the wounded. While so engaged, a grape-shot killed the father and carried off the son's leg. Amputation had been performed, and he was, they said, "doing well." Doing well! When I saw him, he seemed to be asleep. It was piteous to see his sad, pale face, rosy with health but two days ago, now showing sorrow and suffering even in sleep. No one had been to see him or inquire after him. Poor child! I suppose, then, he has no mother, and is an orphan indeed. What a sorrowful beginning of life for him! Perhaps he was the eldest of the family, proud of having in charge his motherless brothers and sisters, and being able to work for them. Think of those little ones in their cottage, waiting and wondering why father and brother do not come home at sunset. How war scatters its miseries, farther and wider than its grape-shot, over the quiet happy fields!

There was one man in hospital the bones of whose hand had been splintered by a bullet. He looked as vivacious as if nothing had happened to him. He was a Venetian, had escaped to Piedmont, entered the service there, was disgusted at not having the medal for the war of '59, and so deserted to join Garibaldi and fight for the liberation of his native town. He said that his only regret was, that he had not had a chance of killing one of the enemy before he was wounded himself, and of washing his hands in his blood. And he said the terrible words, "Lavar mi le mani nel suo sangue," with the sweetest of smiles, as when a gourmet speaks of some favourite dainty. While I was there, Colonel da Porta, a Sicilian commanding his battalion, came in, and filled the man with delight by announcing his nomination as sottotenente (ensign).

The field ambulance of this strange army is under the direction of a Piedmontese lady, the Contessa della T., who attracted great attention in Naples (which, without being uncharitable, one may suppose was not displeasing to her) by the singularity of her manners, language, and costume. She was dressed in a white braided hussar tunic, trousers, and boots outside, with spurs, and a Spanish hat with plumes, and a sword which clanked as she walked in an alarming way. She was attended by three or four Calabrians, dressed like the conventional brigands of the stage, who served as her body-guard. She talked in all languages, and somewhat took off the grace of her charitable deeds by blowing a trumpet so loudly before her.*

In returning, we visited the palace of Caserta. No one was permitted to enter the gardens without an order, which we had some difficulty in procuring. I was referred from one general to another, all royally lodged in the palace ; at last General Medici was good enough to let us pass through his apartments on the ground floor.

The arrangement of the gardens resembles that of the gardens at La Granja in Spain, only on a much larger scale. An aqueduct conveys a copious stream of water to the side of a steep ilex-clothed hill about two miles off, at the back of the palace. Thence it descends first in a natural waterfall over rough rocks, and afterwards in small cascades alternating with still pools, to the plain. From the foot of the waterfall to the palace the distance is 3100 yards. Avenues of ilex and other trees bound the terraces on either side, and there is an abundance of statues, gods, men, dolphins, monsters, and grottoes. At the foot of the waterfall are two groups in marble, representing on one side Diana and her nymphs, on the other, Actæon torn by his hounds, all reflected in the dark deep water. The rocks about are clothed with acacia, oleander, and aloe. In the largest pool was a shoal of old carp and one stately swan, which, accustomed to be fed by royal hands, came sailing up to ask for biscuit of the intruders. From the highest terrace is a beautiful and singular view. You look over the palace and the densely wooded level plain in which it lies, like a dark green sea, beyond the rim of which rise the highlands of Capri, and the Punta di Sorrento.

The palace itself is more than 200 yards square,† if my

---

* When a lady chooses to dress and behave like a man, she forfeits the immunities of her sex, and it is no longer ungallant to criticise her actions.

† Vanvitelli, the architect, published a description of the palace in 1756, from which it appears that the outer sides measure respectively 920 and 720 Neapolitan palms. A copy of this rare work is found—as, indeed, what rare book is not?—in the library at Keir.

rough measurement be right, and is divided into four courts, with an open arcade occupying the ground floor from gate to gate. A broad staircase, lined with costly marbles, leads to a great octagon hall occupying the centre of the pile, with four windows at the angles looking each into a separate court. The octagon is supported by pillars of African marble taken from the temple of Serapis at Puzzuoli. All the palaces I have ever seen yield in magnificence to this ; Versailles is *mesquin* in comparison. What would Ferdinand have said had he lived to see it occupied by a rabble of revolutionary troops, lighting camp fires in the centre of his courts, cooking, playing cards, smoking, and singing Garibaldi's hymn? I can easily conceive that the generals who are enjoying royal luxuries, and exercising among them more than royal power, are not anxious for the arrival of Victor Emmanuel, who would relegate them to some less sumptuous abode, and to some inferior position.

When I reached the railway-station, I found a train of empty trucks and cattle waggons just starting. A number of the red-shirted gentry demanded that a carriage should be attached to it for their use. The station-master declared he had none, whereupon they threatened, hustled, and collared him, and finally carried him off to the palace, to answer to some one for his contumacy. This is one instance among many of the insolence which has made the liberators more unpopular at Naples than ever were its former masters.

The train started without waiting for the issue of the dispute. I got upon a truck with a number of common soldiers (Garibaldians), whose behaviour presented a very favourable contrast to that of their officers. One provided me with an inverted basket to sit upon, another compelled me to accept a cigar (very bad, it is true, but the best he had), a third insisted upon my taking a cartridge as a keepsake. One of them had been an artist, he told me, and had abandoned his easel at Milan to carry a musket in Calabria.

Never, surely, was there such a motley army as this. It

contains men of all ranks, and of all characters; there are men of high birth and gentle breeding, there are also outcasts and vagabonds; there are generous and chivalrous enthusiasts, there are also charlatans and impostors, and unhappily it is not always the former who fill the highest places.

I have seldom seen any earthly object arrayed in such glory as was Vesuvius in the splendour of that calm evening. Through vistas of vine-clad poplars we saw the cone all ruddy purple, every furrow in the outer shell of the mountain distinctly marked with blue shadows, which deepened towards its base into the richest ultramarine. The more recent lava-streams were (like the cone) of a bright purple, and looked, to my fancy, like piles of grapes poured out, waiting for the winepress that should extract from them the famous Vesuvian product—Lacryma Christi.

The name Lacryma Christi, by the way, which shocks English ears, at least when translated, is an instance of the familiarity, and, as it seems to us, irreverence with which Italians treat sacred persons and things. I remember to have read a lecture of Dr. Newman's, in which he maintained the thesis, that the profane and blasphemous oaths habitually used by the people in Italy, proved that the objects of devotion were always present to their minds in whatever aspect, and that the state of mind of an Italian was far preferable to the apathy and indifference of the lower orders in England. To this one might reply on behalf of our countrymen, that their favourite expletive, by the same reasoning, proves the thought of eternal salvation to be always present to their minds. Again, Dr. Newman's proposition would lead to the further inference that a man is religious at heart in proportion to the profanity of his language, "which is absurd," as Euclid says. Again, many of the Italian oaths are obscene. Dr. Newman would find it difficult to twist this fact into an argument for their purity of mind. In some, too, which he who has once heard would gladly forget, profanity and obscenity are combined to form a result which outrages every good feeling. Remembering these, one can only think of Dr. Newman's argument with disgust, as something more than disingenuous.

All men of education in Southern Italy disclaim any sympathy with the religion of the lower orders, which is mere paganism disguised under new names, and consists in the worship of a number of local deities. The Madonna of one shrine is, in the popular imagination—for it is not definite enough to be called a creed—quite a different person from the Madonna of another.

The friar who tends the little chapel at the entrance of the Grotto of Puzzuoli begged one day of a passing stranger, "for the Madonna." " La Reina degli Angeli è ricca abbastanza," said the stranger. " Ah ! bah ! " said the friar, " non à mica la Reina degli Angeli ! è la *povera* Madonna della Grotta, che le manca anche per pagare l'olio " (she has not enough to pay for the oil to light the lamps of the tunnel).

A friend among many good stories told me one, *ben trovato*, if not *vero*, which illustrates the primitive simplicity of their faith. A woman at Naples, praying the Madonna to come and heal her son, took care to give her address—"Vieni, Maria, vieni, numero tredici, vicolo della Scrofa, terzo piano, seconda porta a man destra."

Nowhere, probably, in the world is the separation so great between the well-to-do classes and the poor as it is in South Italy. They are quite distinct in religion, thought, and feeling. Between the highest and the lowest there is, indeed, outwardly a familiarity of manner which, at first sight, would point to an opposite conclusion. We see none of the hauteur on the one side, or the servility on the other, which is so common in England; but the familiarity is only superficial and apparent. There is a deep unfathomed gulf fixed between those who have something and those who have nothing to lose. A householder or shopkeeper at Naples speaks of the lazzaroni as a Hindoo living beside a jungle might speak of the tigers. So there is probably no country in the world where the opinion of the middle and upper classes is so fallacious a test of the popular opinion. The newspaper controversies and the theatre-riots of Naples only indicate the division of opinion in the middle and upper ranks—some holding with Victor Emmanuel, some with Mazzini, some with Cavour, some with Garibaldi—but they tell us nothing of the sentiments of the masses. The mob of the towns, the priests and the peasantry, are probably more inclined, by this time, to the old than to the new Government. If you asked a *contadino* his opinion early in September, the answer was always to the same effect : " Rè Vittorio, Rè Giuseppe, Rè Francesco," it is all one provided he gives us " da mangiare à buon mercato." And when they find that prices are enhanced instead of lowered, under the new reign, they will be sure to throw the blame on the Government. I do not doubt that if universal suffrage were honestly applied to test the opinion of Southern Italy, a large majority would be found for Francesco II., at least in the Abruzzi and the provinces adjacent to the capital. Cavour threw a slur on his master's cause, and made a flaw in his claim, by resting it on a successful repetition of that French juggling imposture, which is as discreditable to statesmen as the miracle of San Gennaro is to priests. The intelligence of a country should rule it and determine its destinies ; and if all the intelligence be, as in South Italy, centred in one class, that class should alone be called upon to give its suffrage.

*Sept.* 22.—The last news I heard before leaving Naples was, that Garibaldi's " moderate " Ministry had resigned in a body, and that a set of Red Republicans had succeeded them. People are beginning to fear that in his heart the General wishes for a republic, and that he will play Victor Emmanuel false. After the use he made of the King's name, which has indeed been a tower of strength to him, this would be an act of perfidy without parallel in history. The confidence felt in Garibaldi has, however, been so much shaken, that it is looked upon as a possible contingency. It is reported, that to an aide-de-camp whom the King sent to him two days ago, he said, "Tell your master that if a republic should be necessary, I will do my best to make him Dictator." This doubt of Garibaldi's intentions was evidently felt by the Ministry, who a few days ago insisted upon taking the oath of allegiance to Victor Emmanuel. The Dictator did not take it, probably on the plea that he was already his subject. In three weeks I have seen the extinction of a popularity that seemed boundless. The people who were wild with delight at the arrival of Garibaldi would now be equally delighted to get rid of him. The reasons for this change are obvious. His refusal to declare at once the annexation of Southern Italy to Northern has alienated the moderate party, and generated suspicion of his intentions, which his violent language on several occasions has tended to confirm. In his proclamation to the Palermitans, he said that he would proclaim Italian unity from the top of the Quirinal only—thus menacing even France. In an order of the day lamenting the death of one of his officers, he praised him for being a true democrat ; in a letter to one Brusco, published in the official journal, he proclaimed his irreconcileable hostility to the men who had humiliated the national dignity and sold an Italian province. All this has created a feeling that he is dragging Naples on, not towards a peaceful union with the rest of Italy, but towards an abyss of anarchy and war. Again, many of the decrees issued by him far outstep the limits of a confessedly temporary and transitional power. He declares the royal property to be national property—he banishes the Jesuits and confiscates their goods—he does the like to the most eminent prelates— he abolishes State lotteries—he forbids the payment of *gamorra* —he concedes the right of fishing in the ports—all which may be useful measures, but not necessary to be done at once (unless the banishment of the prelates be regarded as a measure of security). These and a number of other measures might be left to the consideration of the regular Government. His nomination of Alexander Dumas to be director of the national museum, offended all men of education. The offence **was** increased by the summary dismissal, without compensation, of all the *employés* of the museum, and by a paper issued by the new director full of insolence and arrogance, in which he told the Neapolitans that want of education had degraded them to the level of brutes, and that he was about to raise them by showing them all that was great in politics and beautiful in art. If this offended the upper classes, the seizing of the carriages yesterday was a measure which has still more deeply offended the lower—not the owners and drivers alone, but others who see that their rights of property may be any day similarly invaded. Add to these causes of complaint, the bullying and insolent demeanour of many of Garibaldi's officers, and the natural reaction and discouragement which could not but follow such a fever of excitement, and we shall see enough to account for the decline of his popularity. "I'll make you a bet," said a Neapolitan to me, "that his power will not last as long as Masaniello's." "Que venga il Re Vittorio Emmanuele e venga subito, con venti mila soldati per cacciarci da Napoli questa canaglia!" was the fervid exclamation of another who had made himself hoarse with shouting "Viva Garibaldi" on the 7th of September.

Garibaldi's character was thus summed up by a friend of mine at Turin: "He is a brave soldier, but a great fool," using the phrase (I suppose) in the sense of "un grand fou." I thought it harsh at the time, but my Neapolitan friends, chiefly belonging to the "moderate" party, were agreed in thinking it not so far from the truth. He was of course the chief topic of conversation during my stay at Naples. I give, in as few words as I can, the residuum of much talk.

As a soldier, he is of undaunted courage and a master of the "dodges" (passez-moi le mot) which are required in guerilla war, but he has no conception of a general's duties in the field ; he is ignorant of the very rudiments of tactics, and incapable of organization on a large scale. He is kind and gentle in his manners, and reluctant to hurt any one's feelings, while he is reckless of their lives. His bravery and gentleness, his generosity and disinterestedness, secure him the personal affection of all around him, and that constitutes

his great merit as a commander. He pushes his love of
simplicity to a point bordering on affectation, and is almost
ostentatious in his dislike of pomp. He is illogical, pre-
judiced, and obstinate to a degree never before combined. He
thinks cavalry useless, and has a profound contempt for
cannon. He is perfectly certain that he has only to appear
before the walls of Rome, and the French will leave it, taking
with them the Holy Father. " What if they don't ? " it was
urged. " O, but they will !" was the answer, in the tone of a
man who admits no further discussion. He thinks that the
walls of Mantua and Verona will fall, like those of Jericho,
at a shout. He is very easily imposed on, and believes in all
those who are about him. Familiarity breeds respect, and no
proof will convince him of the dishonesty of any one whom
he has once trusted. He has not the moral courage to say
" No " to a request of any of these favourites. His ignorance
is such that the smallest show of knowledge completely im-
poses upon him. He thinks Crespi a statesman, and Dumas
a scholar. However, in forming an estimate of him, as of
other extraordinary characters in history, we ought to be on
our guard against the tendency natural to men to reduce emi-
nence to the ordinary level by discovering a number of small
failings. And when all abatements are made, there remain
the great facts. His achievements are to be accounted for.
He alone had gauged correctly the real weakness of the
Neapolitan power, and the strength of his own seemingly
feeble means, and he had the courage to test practically the
truth of his conclusions. His life-long devotion to one great
idea, and his strength of will, have made him " a king of
men," and distinguish him from the crowd, who are always,
on their own showing, victims to " circumstances over which
they have no control."

I left Naples for Civita Vecchia on the afternoon of this
day. On board the steamer I met General Bosco. He
was prevented by illness from following the army to Capua,
and was in Naples when Garibaldi arrived. The latter

has required or advised him to leave the country for a while :
he is therefore going to Paris. He says that all the arrangements for the equipment and feeding of the Neapolitan
troops are very good ; that, in general, the material order of
the army is excellent, but that the late King ruined its *morale*
by introducing a system of promotion which has neither the
advantages of the Austrian nor of the French system. The
officers are not, as in the Austrian army, taken from the upper
classes in society, and who therefore command the respect of
the soldiers, and have, or ought to have, a nice sense of personal honour ; neither are they, as in the French army, chosen
in great measure from among the bravest and most intelligent
men in the ranks ; but they are men without either social
rank or individual merit. As far as I could understand, promotion is made by seniority, and is excessively slow. There
were some men, he said, still lieutenants at fifty. Most of
these old officers are married men and very poor, having little
or nothing but their pay to live on, so that their interests and
anxieties are with their families and not with the regiment,
and thus *ces pères de famille* are capable of any treason or
baseness if only they can avoid exposing lives so valuable at
home. In the higher grades, of course, exceptions are made.
General Bosco's own case is an instance. He was only a major
at the accession of the present King—if I may still call
Francesco II. "the present King."

Between the police-office, the custom-house, and the railway-station, a traveller's patience is sorely tried at Civita
Vecchia, as might be expected, seeing that there is in
prescribing formalities a most elaborate system, and in exe-
cuting them no system at all. One who knows Rome
well tells me that utter confusion reigns in all the depart-
ments of administration, from the highest to the lowest. In
their normal state, the Government offices are like what they
were in England, in the days when Samuel Pepys was at the
Admiralty ; just now they are in the condition which the said
offices must have been in after the news of William's landing

at Torbay had reached the metropolis. In the best of times every official pilfers quietly, in proportion to his rank ; now there is a general scramble.

I was eager to see Rome in this supreme crisis of its fortunes. I find that the crisis is like that of a fever, through which the patient passes in unconsciousness. It is said that there is a committee, or committees, somewhere, in communication with the revolutionists at Genoa and Naples ; but no one seems to know or care anything about it. At Naples, in the last days of Francesco, the committees kept issuing, three or four times a day, bulletins of news and inflammatory placards ; here I see nothing of the kind. People in the *cafés* talk about the movements of the Piedmontese without fear or restraint ; but also, as it seems to me, without interest or sympathy. I see " Viva Garibaldi !" " Viva Vittorio Emmanuele !" scribbled on the walls ; but these inscriptions are apparently of old date, and the police have not taken the trouble to efface them—perhaps the most effectual way of neutralising their effect, just as the Irish denunciations of English tyranny are perpetually contradicted by the fact that they are allowed to be expressed. I see no groups, as at Naples, gathered round some one who has the latest news to tell. We are in complete ignorance as to what is going on at Ancona or Capua. We do not even know for certain where the nearest outposts of the Piedmontese army lie. All communications are interrupted, and the latest intelligence is conveyed in private letters from Turin or Paris. If, however, the people here were not indifferent, we should surely hear a great deal of false news and reports, originating in excited imaginations.

The *Giornale di Roma*—the only paper allowed to be printed—gives us news from Shanghai, and a discussion as to whether the Matilda of Dante was an Italian Princess or a German Saint, but contains not a word of news respecting the invading army. It was so with the Government organ at Naples in the last days of Francesco   Meanwhile, every one believes that the days of the Pope's reign, as a temporal sovereign, are numbered. The *dénouement* is certain, in whatever way it may be brought about. We who look on are like the reader of a novel who has peeped at the last page and seen that it ends happily, so that he goes through the book with diminished interest, but with some curiosity nevertheless to see by what ingenious process the author will extricate his characters from their embarrassment.

The conduct of the plot is no doubt all settled between the great *collaborateurs* at Turin and Paris. The Romans, in the meantime, are not at all sorry to let other people play their game, and give effect to their wishes, without being involved in the risk and worry of an insurrection :

> " If fate will have me king, why fate may crown me
> Without my stir."

When a man can lie at his ease while other people climb the tree to shake the ripe fruit down to the ground within his reach, who can wonder at his acquiescence in so comfortable an arrangement?

The Holy Father, it is said, remains at the Vatican, freed from most of the cares of government; eating heartily and sleeping soundly, cheerfully preparing himself for the scaffold or the stake, thus enjoying by anticipation all the glories of martyrdom, together with a comfortable assurance that he will not be called upon to endure the pain thereof.

An ardent Protestant asked the English clergyman the other day, "What arrangements he had made in the event of the fall of the Papacy?" expecting, I suppose, that he would put on his surplice and bands, and, followed by his clerk proceed to read himself in at St. Peter's according to the form prescribed in the Book of Common Prayer.

There is a very general idea prevalent, both among the foes and the friends of the Pope, that the destruction of his temporal will entail the ruin of his spiritual power. Among Protestants the wish is father to the thought, and the impatient interpreters of prophecy find no warrant in their texts for breaking the fall of Antichrist half-way down.

Among devout Romanists the notion arises from their attach-
ment to the tradition of their Church, which holds the two
powers to be inseparable, and which clutches at the sub-
stantial patrimony of St. Peter with as much tenacity as
his metaphorical keys.  In reality, I doubt whether ardent
anti-Romanists are wise in advocating the abolition of the
temporal power.  The notorious scandals of the Papal
administration tend to throw a slur upon his spiritual
pretensions.  If a man know not how to rule his own house-
hold, how shall he rule the Church of Christ ?  How can the
worst of temporal sovereigns be the best of spiritual fathers ?

I believe that his position as spiritual sovereign would
be strengthened by the abolition of the temporal power.  It
is a reform as urgently needed as the reforms which were
brought about within the Roman Church after Luther's
secession.  From those reforms the Church derived new
strength and a fresh lease of existence.  That lease is now
run out, and can only be renewed on condition of parting
with the temporal power.  The world is not yet ripe for the
destruction of the spiritual domination, and till then the
powers of Napoleon, and Victor Emmanuel, and Garibaldi
all united will not prevail against it.  Not martyr flames
nor trenchant swords shall do away that ancient institution.

*Sept.* 23.—The gardens of the French Academy on the Pin-
cian, open to the public this (Sunday) afternoon, are planted
in a manner rather unusual now-a-days.  Narrow walks
intersect each other at right angles, bordered on each side by
tall hedges of box overtopped by ilex and bay (here meriting
its name of *laurus nobilis*), with generally at each angle a
cypress or pine.  Such a garden, delightfully cool and pleasant beneath this Italian sun, would be damp, and chill,
and mouldy in England.  Nevertheless the lieges of Elizabeth
used to love "pleached alleys," and I could fancy that
Shakespeare planted for himself some such "trim plea-
saunce" at New Place.  I wonder if there was more sunshine
in England in those days.  In Spenser and Shakespeare
it is almost always sunshine—a notable storm now and then

—but sunshine as a rule. Is there any truth in the fancy of all old people that the weather used to be warmer and finer when they were young? Or is it that nature has kindly provided for men, whether poets or not, that only the sunny hours of life shall make a lasting impression on the memory, like the dial that says, "Horas non numero nisi serenas?"

In sight of the stone bench where I am sitting are a group of children, from twelve to fifteen years old, playing with a heartiness which we are accustomed to think a special characteristic of English children. It is a sunny hour for them. Their game is called Ladri e Sbirri. The first thing they do is to stand round in a ring. Each holds out three fingers. The biggest boy counts, beginning from his left hand, three, six, nine, &c. up to twenty-one, after which he goes on counting each boy as one till he gets to thirty-one, and number thirty-one is the Capo Sbirro. This elaborate device is to prevent cheating in the choice of a leader. The Capo Ladro is chosen in the same way. The head spy and the head robber then choose their men alternately. The Sbirri tie a handkerchief for distinction round the left arm, and start in chase of the robbers. Some of the stone seats are supposed, "by making believe very much," to be caves, where they are secure. If the robbers succeed in escaping all to the same cave, they win the game. It was curious to observe how, even in the ardour of the game, the slow, *traînant*, distinct enunciation of the Romans was preserved. A strange contrast to the confused gibberish of the Neapolitans.

*Sept.* 25.—The Pope had ordered solemn prayers for three days—a *triduo* is the name still in use, adopted like so many others from Pagan Rome—to be offered for the success of his arms. These were repeated for three successive evenings at vesper time, in one of the chapels of St. Peter's. Swiss guards lined each side of the chapel, and the Holy Father himself, in scarlet cope, knelt in front of the altar, and once during the ceremony offered incense. The persons present—five or six

hundred in number—joined in the chanting with great apparent fervour, but before the service was over, a large part had
scurried off, and taken their place in a double line leading
to the door, by which his Holiness was to pass on the way
to the Vatican. The Pope looked placid and benignant as
ever, and showed no trace of care or trouble in face or figure.
People dropped on their knees to receive his benediction.

An Englishman, whose Protestantism has been intensified
by residence in Rome, to whom I spoke of the effective performance I had just witnessed, said, "Yes, they are consum-
mate actors, but I have long felt that the play has lost its
attractiveness by too much repetition, and now it is more
dreary to me than ever, for I know that there is no money to
renew the dresses and decorations, or to pay the wages of the
scene-shifters and candle-snuffers."

Early in October I returned by way of Marseilles and Paris.
All the Frenchmen I talked with on the steamer and in the
railway carriage showed great irritation against Italians in
general, and Garibaldi in particular. They were very sore
about Castelfidardo, and the fate of the Pope's French volunteers, who had fought like lions "*un contre cent,*" and before
succumbing to numbers had annihilated a whole regiment of
Piedmontese. If their opinion could be taken as an index of
the general feeling of France, the Emperor would be taking a
popular course if he were to restore the *status quo* in Italy by
force of arms, leaving only Lombardy to Piedmont, as a compensation for Savoy and Nice. It was agreed that the position of Austria in Venice was intolerable. "*Que faire?*" My
suggestion that Austria should sell it was ridiculed as "*une
idée vraiment Anglaise,*"* they not seeming to remember that
the great Napoleon netted a good round sum by a similar
transaction with regard to Louisiana.

These same Frenchmen showed, I am sorry to say, no good
will towards England. They spoke out their sentiments with

* Now (December, 1860), this very plan is recommended by several journals
in France, as the only solution of the difficulty.

that complete disregard of a stranger's feelings which dis-
tinguishes them from all other nations, and makes them
essentially the rudest nation in Europe. They told me that
every one knew the great ultimate purpose of the Emperor's
policy was the humiliation of England; that in less than
ten years he would take Gibraltar from us, and give it to
Spain, he would take the Ionian Islands and give them to
Greece, thus making allies for himself everywhere at our
expense; that he would seize Egypt, and cut us off from India,
&c. &c.

A countryman whom I met at Paris had been the object of
similar polite attentions in crossing France. One of his fellow-
travellers, rejoicing in the prospect of a speedy war, rubbed
his hands and said with a cheerful smile, " Oui, Monsieur,
nous vous mangerons les entrailles."

The French say, and by constantly affirming it have half-
persuaded themselves, that they are stronger than we, and
would, in the event of a war, be certainly victorious, but
beneath their boasting lurks a feeling of distrustful fear, which
will give them pause, and make them reflect that they may
find a cheaper and safer way of gratifying their national
vanity by continuing to brag of what they will do than by
trying to do it.